Parachuting to Danger

Parachuting to Danger

A British Airman with the French Resistance

LIONEL SCOTT

To Geoffrey,

With my best wishes.

Lionel Scott

ROBERT HALE · LONDON

© *Lionel Scott 1959 and 1988*
Originally published 1959 as 'I Dropped In'
This revised edition 1988

Robert Hale Limited
Clerkenwell House
Clerkenwell Green
London EC1R 0HT

British Library Cataloguing in Publication Data

Scott, Lionel
    Parachuting to danger : a British airman
    with the French Resistance.—2nd ed.
    1. France. British anti-German espionage,
    1939–1945. Biographies
    I. Title   II Scott, Lionel. I dropped in
    940.54'86'410924

ISBN 0-7090-3528-4

Photoset in Baskerville by
Derek Doyle & Associates, Mold, Clwyd.
Printed in Great Britain by
St Edmundsbury Press, Bury St Edmunds, Suffolk
on acid-free Supreme Antique Wove
supplied by Silverton Mill and bound by
WBC Bookbinders Ltd.

Illustrations

Between pages 96 and 97

PICTURE CREDITS

Aeroplane Monthly: 2. Imperial War Museum: 4–5, 7–10. All
other illustrations in the collection of the author.

Foreword to the new edition

The first draft of this book was prepared in 1949. My original intention was to chronicle the events that occurred after I was shot down into occupied France so that my sons, when they were old enough to understand, would have an account of my adventure. I did not at that time ever consider my story for publication.

It was, however, published thanks to the encouragement of the late Sir Stanley Unwin but not before the copy had been censored by the Air Ministry. At that time I was still an RAF officer, albeit on reserve, so had no alternative but to accept the omission of some material 'that might be helpful to those who are seeking missing parts for their jigsaw'.

Looking back after some forty years I appreciate that some of the excised accounts may then, and even now, have involved national security but one incident in particular had a sinister personal connotation details of which I recount for the first time in Chapter 9 and in the Postscript.

L.S.

Preface

The day after war was declared I joined the Army and became an Officer Cadet. After selection all Officer Cadets were sent home to await posting to OCTU. I was then eighteen years old, and a subsequent decision of the governments that no one under nineteen years of age would be sent overseas resulted in my training being deferred until after my nineteenth birthday. I tried to transfer to the RAF but at that time it was not possible to do so.

In May 1940 Hitler marched into the Lowlands. The bombing of London, the Dunkirk evacuation, and the invasion scare all followed, and the only contribution I made to the war effort was to attach myself to the Local Defence Volunteers and stand pike in hand guarding Richmond Waterworks. I was now nineteen, but still the Army did not call me. Repeated visits to the War Office and innumerable letters produced no results, until one morning a communication arrived granting me permission to apply for aircrew duties in the RAF. I applied and in due course was told to report for medical examination and selection board interview. It is from that moment that my story begins, though this book deals primarily with my experiences while evading capture in Northern France.

Let me end this preface by saying that this is a true story. It has not been fictionalized. The truth of nearly every main incident can be verified. Even if we should disagree as to the personal motives involved, or interpret differently the causes of events, the simple truth of the incidents remains.

I should like to explain my choice of the word 'evadee'.

An 'evadee' was an airman who, having been shot down

over enemy occupied territory, had succeeded in avoiding capture by evading the enemy. An 'escaper', on the other hand, was an airman who had been taken prisoner and had subsequently escaped. The RAF Escaping Society (while accepting both successful escapers and evadees as members) recognizes the difference between these two groups, and uses the term 'evadee'. I quote them as my authority should the reader be unable to find the word in a dictionary.

One

'Is there an L. R. Scott here?' asked the medical orderly.

The corporal passed on the question and I confirmed my presence.

'You haven't left us a sample of your water,' he said. 'The MO is proper chokker. Come with me.'

I followed him sheepishly whilst the ranks behind me tittered.

The MO was waiting.

'Are you Scott?'

'Yes, sir.'

'What do you mean by going without leaving a sample?'

'No one asked me to, sir.'

'You mean no one gave you one of these?' He held up a glass measure.'

'No, sir.'

'Oh, all right. Take this. When you've finished give it to the nurse and rejoin your squad; and be quick about it, they're waiting for you.'

I took the jar and looked round the room.

'In there,' he snapped impatiently. 'Hurry up.'

I stepped into a small cubicle, and attempted to oblige him. Nothing happened. A minute passed, then two, then three. Sheer panic struck me. I dared not emerge with an empty jar. What could I do?

The MO's face came round the corner.

'What's the matter?'

'I can't do anything, sir.'

'Oh, for heaven's sake! Bring him a glass of water, nurse.'

A WAAF nurse appeared carrying a glass of water.

Quickly adjusting my dress I emerged from the cubicle

and took the glass in my right hand, still holding the measure in my left. Her face was quite expressionless, but as I raised the glass to my lips she said, 'Cheers.'

I emptied the glass, handed it back, and, consumed with embarrassment, dived into the cubicle, but still nothing happened. I could now hear giggling and someone said, 'Perhaps if we whistled.'

I looked round helplessly. There was no escape, so plucking up all my courage I emerged and with as much dignity as I could muster started to say:

'I'm sorry, but ...'

The MO stopped me.

'Look, old chap,' he said, in a much kinder tone. 'Take another drink of water, go into the washroom, turn on a tap and leave it running, take your shoes and socks off and walk about on the stone floor.'

I took his advice and soon was able to rejoin my squad. The corporal said nothing; he just shook his head from side to side. All the way down the long corridors I marched to a chorus of ribald whispers.

We sat down. The test papers were set before us. I was suffering so much from embarrassment that I was incapable of doing myself justice. Quite simple arithmetical problems found me confused and jumpy. When the papers were collected I knew I had done badly.

Outside the corporal dismissed us, and called me over. 'Don't go on the beer tonight, old son,' he said, 'because if you have the same trouble again you might burst.'

The following morning we paraded at Euston House and the names of those who had been passed as fit for flying duties were read out. Mine was among them.

However, my jubilation was short-lived, for the chairman of the selection board told me that because of an astigmatism of the left eye I could never be a pilot. He went on to say that my examination papers were not up to the standard they would have expected from one with my education. I could hardly explain the reasons for my poor showing without giving an account of my medical, and I was not prepared to do this.

The three members of the board then questioned me on a variety of subjects. I must have acquitted myself fairly well, for it was eventually suggested that I go home and brush up on my maths with a view to becoming a navigator. I did not want to do any more waiting, so they accepted me as a wireless-operator air-gunner. This was a foolish decision of mine, for the educational standard required of a prospective navigator was well within my capabilities, and navigators being scarce they began their training almost immediately.

This was not so where wireless operators were concerned. They had many months of waiting before they could hope to reach a signals school, and then were posted to a station as ground operators before being called to gunnery school. By the time I became a wireless operator the interval between the two schools had become so great that it had been found necessary to institute refresher courses for operators before they could proceed for gunnery training. All this took considerable time, but then, how was I to know?

It took me nearly two years to become a wireless-operator air-gunner; nearly two years of frustration, disappointment, and sometimes despair. From the beginning it was made plain to me that wireless-operator air-gunners under training were the hand-maidens of the pelican Air Force, and that no task was too menial for them, nor any duty sufficiently hard.

We were bullied and harried, driven from task to task with a ruthlessness and enthusiasm so great that, directed towards the war effort, it would have merited the greatest approbation. It was difficult to understand the attitude of our NCOs. No crime was on our heads but that of having volunteered to fly and fight. Yet in their eyes this was a crime. We were living reminders that there were other people, and their mean little world admitted none save those who crept beneath the shelter of their rank, who measured success by the lightness of their duties and failure by being found out.

It always amused them to give us the dirtiest fatigues and they made no secret of the fact that we were being mildly victimized. I remember arriving at RAF station Evanton, a lonely place, twenty-eight miles north of Inverness. To get there, our party of about twenty 'sprog' airmen had travelled from Bournemouth. The journey had taken thirty-six hours. It need not have taken quite so long, but the corporal in charge of us had wanted to visit his girl friend in Swindon and had arranged our route to make this possible. Anyway, there we stood, tired, dirty and dishevelled, apprehensively surveying our new station and its impressive warrant officer. After listening to, and accepting, some explanation from our NCO as to why we were late, he came over and beamed at us good-naturedly. 'Welcome to RAF station Evanton, gentlemen,' he said. 'We are pleased to accept you into our company.' We were so overcome by his affability, and so tired by our journeying, that we fell for it, hook, line and sinker, and beamed back at him.

'Take those stupid grins off your miserable faces,' he roared. 'I'll give you something to grin at, you lousy shower. Let me tell you: trainee aircrew are dirt so far as I'm concerned and before you leave here you'll wish you'd never joined.'

Shocked out of our wits we stood at attention while he walked up and down our ranks eyeing each and every one of us with an expression of disdain. He stopped in front of me.

'What's your name?' he snapped.

'Scott, sir,' I said.

'Come again! What do you call yourself?'

'My name is Scott, sir,' I said.

He affected an exaggerated accent.

'Oh! Your name is Scott, is it?' He pondered for a moment. 'Well, Scott, old man, I have a little job for you. Corporal!' he shouted at the top of his voice, and his stooge came running. 'Corporal, put this refined young man on the coal cart.'

This was the beginning of a new life, in which my accent was responsible for the cleanliness of many a latrine.

I endured everything that came my way and did my best to perform even the most onerous tasks as efficiently as possible. Indeed, I took a stubborn delight in showing my persecutors that their worst was not enough to break my spirit, though there were times when I felt very lonely. My nickname was 'Happy'.

One day, whilst working on the coal cart, I chanced to speak to the padre at the Church of Scotland canteen. We had just delivered his coal, and in appreciation he invited us in for a cup of tea. We talked about this and that and told him of our plight: that we were aircrew waiting posting for training, meantime employed on general duties. He suggested that we might like to come to the canteen in the evenings and assist his women helpers. It was rewarding work, he said, and might lead to our being welcomed into local homes. My companions were not over-enthusiastic, but I jumped at the chance, and spent many happy hours thereby. I soon knew people in the village, and their kindness and friendship did much to alleviate the miserable existence that had been mine until then.

Eventually we were posted to Blackpool and began our training. Life was now much more bearable, for dance-halls and cinemas prevented boredom in the evenings and our work was interesting during the day. After Blackpool came Yatesbury, where we qualified as wireless operators. Instead of going on to gunnery school we were – due to bottlenecks in training – posted to ground stations, ostensibly as operators, though in fact many went back to general duties. For the first time since joining the service I was lucky, being posted to Croydon, only a bicycle ride away from my home in Richmond.

For six months I did practically nothing. The signals section was so overstaffed that a couple of hours' work a day by every man was more than enough to maintain its efficiency. Added to all this we were billeted in empty private houses with literally no supervision.

When we went back to Yatesbury for our refresher course we needed it!

I remember Yatesbury for two reasons. The first, the frequency with which sausages appeared, due to the camp's proximity to Harris's of Calne. The second, a comic-opera performance which took place at the end of each working day. When classes were over, we would march as a squad to a place of dismissal near our billets. Our route, indeed the route of every squad, was lined with general-duty NCOs. Their task – and I suppose it was a duty ordered by some well-meaning individual – was to see that discipline was maintained and that we marched properly. Their method was to stand glaring angrily at us and to shout hysterically at the tops of their voices. It was extremely difficult to run this gauntlet without grinning. I suppose they made some other contribution to the war effort.

I mention these facts to contrast the feelings and sentiments of those around us when we were training with the wonderful spirit that existed between all ranks in an operational squadron, and particularly between the men who flew the planes and the men who kept them flying.

I have often wondered how such extremes of attitude could exist in the RAF. Admittedly, these general-duty men were the poorest paid and least qualified members of a technical service and felt their position acutely; like many ground crew they resented the fact that all qualified aircrew were senior NCOs.

When I left Yatesbury for the second time it was to go to Mona, on the Isle of Anglesey, where I passed my gunnery course and received my signals brevet and sergeant's stripes.

I had hoped for a commission, but had to wait until later for this. Few commissions were given to wireless-operator air-gunners; one had to be brilliant or lucky. I was neither.

After nearly two years in the ranks, life as a sergeant was very pleasant. The things that one appreciated most were the home comforts: to be able to eat one's meals off a tablecloth; the amenities of a mess; the freedom to go out in the evenings; and, best of all perhaps, no fatigues. I enjoyed operational training. One quickly made friends and, after becoming a member of a crew, the wonderful feeling of belonging to a team in which every man had a part to play essential to the fighting efficiency of an aircraft bred a comradeship that made a mockery out of my days in Training Command.

We trained on Blenheims, Bostons, Wellingtons, Manchesters and eventually Lancasters. In the autumn of 1943 we finished our training and were posted to 44 Squadron, Dunholm Lodge.

Two

Dunholm is a small village, some five miles out of Lincoln on the Market Rasen road. Its occupants, like so many Lincolnshire folk, had had their lives completely disrupted by the RAF, and bore their misfortune with remarkable stoicism.

The natural flatness of the country, and its closeness to the coast, presented the Air Ministry with a series of ideal sites for the construction of bomber airfields. Indeed the circuits of these airfields were so close together that it was not unusual for an aircraft to land on the wrong field whilst in radio contact with its own control tower. It was no cause for wonder that little consideration had or could have been given to the comforts of those who had not been caught up in the machinery of the war effort, and had therefore the privilege, or misfortune, of remaining at home. No doubt there was eventual compensation for the discomforts they endured, but the continual droning of aircraft engines, the raucous laughter and uncouth behaviour in the village once the pubs closed, must have been distressing for those who remembered the peace and quiet of happier times. I always found the villagers kind and good-humoured and marvelled at their forbearance.

Life on an operational squadron had, despite the risks, many compensations. There was leave every six weeks instead of every three months and, apart from flying there were no duties to perform.

Once your aircraft had been tested you were – provided there were no operations – free to do as you pleased.

Sometimes – though not often – there would be lectures, but apart from this, if you had a little money, Lincoln awaited your pleasure.

The Saracen's Head was a great starting-point for an evening out. So much was this hotel a part of Bomber Command that it was said, with some truth, that the barmaids would give an inquiring stranger the name of the target within half an hour of take-off. The White Hart was also a popular rendezvous, and there were many others.

The dance-halls – as always in war-time – were crowded. And why not? For, after the wine, where else could one find young women and old songs in such profusion.

For about a week at the time of the full moon, operations were suspended as a compliment to the Luftwaffe, and the squadrons flocked into the city. All places of amusement and entertainment were taken over. The cinema managers put up the 'house full' notices; the publicans ran out of beer and girls were in short supply. Competition for their favours was fierce, and many a damsel whose face and figure would have provided adequate protection against a fate worse than death in peace-time was wined and dined and suffered her fate with, let us hope, mutual benefit to all concerned.

Lincoln Cathedral, high on the hill, was a splendid sight in the full moon, standing out in silhouette against the horizon and throwing a great shadow across the town as if it were a protective cloak. I was walking to the bus station one night and, pointing out the Cathedral, drew this analogy.

'Cor,' said my companion, 'you'll be wanting me to take time to look at the flowers next.'

Later that night as I lay in my bunk these words came back to me, and I mused on how basic was our existence. We flew when bidden; fed when hungry; slept when tired; prayed when frightened; made love when possible; and satisfied our consciences by blaming war and nature for our deeds and misdeeds. We never made time to look at the flowers.

After completing ten missions I applied for a commission, and during the next few weeks was interviewed in turn by my Signals Leader, my Flight Commander, the Station Adjutant, the Station Commander and, finally, the Air Commodore at Waddington, whose wing included 44 Squadron. I had meanwhile completed another five missions, and with fifteen operations behind me, six of them to Berlin and the shortest one to Brunswick, was half-way through my tour.

Normally a tour of operations consisted of thirty missions, after which a man was rested, usually by being sent to an operational training unit as an instructor. Sometimes he would return for a second tour, which meant another twenty missions, after which a DFC and a decent posting was the normal reward.

I returned from leave on 25 February, 1944, to learn that my commission had been granted and would be gazetted within the next few days. I also learnt that we were on operations that night, so any celebrations would have to be postponed.

There were seven of us in the crew.

Flying Officer Ernie Bartlett, the pilot and captain, was a widower in his early thirties. A quiet, rather sad man, he lived for his twelve-year-old son and would rush off to the Isle of Wight to see him whenever possible. None of us knew him very well, but he was a fine pilot, thorough down to the smallest detail, and very cool in action.

Our navigator, Frank Sturges, was a flight sergeant who had joined us after our first trip, when our original navigator had lost his way to such an extent that we had bombed Stuttgart an hour late, and alone. Somehow we had survived the violent attention of the entire anti-aircraft defences and limped home; but the Wing Commander wisely decided that he badly needed further training. Frank had been on several operations before joining us. He had lost his crew when sickness had prevented him from flying one night, and had been a spare man on the squadron for some time. It was a revelation to fly with him after our experiences with his nervous and slow-working predecessor.

Our bomb-aimer was Sergeant Jack Hoad. Jack was only thirty years old but was already bald. This fact, with his somewhat corpulent figure and a round, red, cheerful face, gave him the appearance of a merry monk. I always felt that he would look more in character gracing an advertisement for Chartreuse than inhabiting the bomb-aimer's compartment in the nose of a Lancaster. He was a most conscientious dropper of bombs, however, and once he got his eye over the bomb-sight was oblivious to everything save the immediate job. Several times we had to make a second run over the target before he would release the bombs. This was an agonizing experience for the crew, for we could only watch the ack-ack and wait. He came in for a good deal of banter on the way home, the two gunners being particularly hard on him.

Our engineer, Harry Middleton, was a regular. He had joined the RAF as a boy apprentice and the Service was his life. He had been a sergeant fitter before remustering to aircrew and was, perhaps, the best-trained flight engineer on the squadron. He was a Geordie, of quiet disposition, thoroughly reliable and most efficient.

Our mid-upper gunner, Joe Swingler, was a Canadian. He had only been in the RCAF a short time. Trained in Canada, he had been on operations within a few months of enlisting, and so had no chips on his shoulder. He was a good crew member; the sort of man who would stay with a friend.

Joe Crawley, our rear gunner, was a Northerner. Joe was married and his wife and home meant everything to him. He hated war and found operations a great strain, yet had volunteered for perhaps the most dangerous job in flying. He had an astringent wit, and was most voluble when circumstances were hazardous. His sense of humour often brought comic relief when most needed.

Our Lancaster was 'A' for 'Able'. 'Able' had completed forty operations when we took her over, and the trip I am going to describe was, I believe, her fifty-seventh. Like a ship, she was very much a 'She', and we looked on her as the only, but much loved, lady of our company.

Three

Briefing was early, for there was to be a daylight take-off. So, shortly after lunch, we assembled in the main briefing room to learn that the target was Augsburg. I say the main briefing room because in practice the individual members of a crew were briefed in their own sections by their respective 'leaders', and then all met for the main briefing, which was in fact a general explanation of the mission. On this particular occasion, however, we were treated to a lengthy homily by the Group Captain, for Augsburg was a target of special significance as far as 44 Squadron was concerned. The late Wing Commander Nettleton – then a squadron leader – had led a magnificent daylight attack on the town, for which he had deservedly been awarded the VC. He had later commanded the squadron, only to be lost over the Bay of Biscay when returning from a Italian raid. The Group Captain reminded us of all this and asked for a special effort.

An hour later we were taxi-ing round the perimeter track waiting to take off. At the end of the operational runway there was a caravan painted with black and white squares like a draughts-board. It was always known as the 'Domino' and housed two or three airmen whose job it was to give the control tower information concerning the state of the runway – whether it was clear of aircraft and so on. They also saw to it that no vehicles crossed the runway when aircraft were landing or taking off. When operations were on, they gave the aircraft their take-off clearance, under telephone instruction from the control tower, by showing a green Aldis lamp. This was done in order to maintain a wireless silence, for the Germans were, of course, listening in on all frequencies.

The aircraft queued up awaiting their turn to take off, and standing looking out of my Perspex dome in the middle of 'A' for 'Able', I had a splendid view of these four-engined monsters, passively awaiting the moment of action.

The Group Captain always parked his car near the 'Domino' and stood at the end of the runway with his driver and perhaps an officer or two. As each pilot opened his engines and moved off, the Group Captain came to attention and saluted; it was a gesture much appreciated by all. Soon our turn came. We swung round on to the runway and cleared our engines. The green Aldis lamp flashed on. Ernie opened the throttles, and we sped off down the runway and up into the darkening sky. I watched the little waving group until they disappeared, and then, sitting down in front of the wireless and radar equipment, opened my log, little knowing that I would never close it.

The first hour after take-off was spent in gaining height, usually over England. This enabled aircraft to cross the enemy coast at about 20,000 feet and lessened the danger from anti-aircraft fire, though not, of course, from fighters.

During this initial and rather boring period, the wireless operator would often tune in to the BBC and play any music being broadcast over the aircraft's intercommunication system. This gave a little innocuous pleasure to everyone before the rigours of the evening.

After the climb, we set course for the target. On the outward part of a mission my duties were limited to logging a half-hourly broadcast from Group Control and passing any information received to the captain, navigator, or bomb-aimer, as the case might be. In between these broadcasts, we used to try to pick up German radio stations which were vectoring fighters on to our bombers. Having tuned in an enemy station, one would 'back tune' the transmitter to the receiver and then, by means of a switch which connected a microphone in one of the engine nacelles to the transmitter, transit this appalling noise on top of the voice of the German controller. Often he could be blotted out in this way, and it was most enjoyable to hear him shouting and swearing as he tried to make himself heard above the din.

Sometimes Group Control would instruct all its aircraft to jam a particular frequency: the ensuing row had to be heard to be believed. It was known as 'tinsling', and I believe most operators performed this duty with relish, for apart from appealing to the malicious 'schoolboy' inherent in all men, it was very much for their own protection. Another very effective defence against fighters was known as the 'window'. Window consisted of small metallized strips of paper which the bomb-aimer dropped from the aircraft at regular intervals. The enemy radar screens were very sensitive to these strips, consequently they caused great interference and made it difficult for the operators to find an aircraft in the showers of window impulses on their screens. Yet a third defence was carried by the aircraft itself – this was 'visual monica'.

Visual monica was a radar device for the detection of enemy fighters. Two aerials, one on the starboard and one on the port side of the tail plane, indicated the presence of any aircraft passing within 600 feet to the rear of the aircraft. These aerials were not sensitive in a forward direction, primarily because the closing speeds of aircraft moving towards one another are too high for a device of limited range to be useful, and also because a pilot will always attack another aircraft from behind if he can, so as to keep it in his sights as long as possible. Once the aerials recorded the presence of an aircraft, two impulses were sent to a cathode ray tube, which projected a 'blip' on to a green radar screen. This screen was divided in two by a calibrated centre line, the impulses of the starboard aerial being recorded on the right of this line and those of the port aerial on the left. The centre line was calibrated from 600 feet at the top, to 200 at the bottom. A 'blip' on the 600-feet marking would be small in diameter, but would increase in size as it moved down the scale, till on the 200-feet mark it would cover the full width of the screen. It is easy to understand, therefore, that if another aircraft were dead astern the two aerials would receive signals of equal strength and the 'blip' would appear on equidistant sides of the central line and move up or down the screen as the distance fluctuated. But should the aircraft move to the port or starboard, one or other of the aerials would receive a stronger signal – because of its greater proximity to the following aircraft. This would be immediately visible on the screen, a bigger 'blip' appearing on one side of the line than the other. It will be appreciated that a 'blip' usually moved off the screen in a few moments. If it remained for long, one warned the gunners, giving its approximate position. Often they would identify it as 'one of ours', and often they would see nothing at all and complain of gadgets that didn't work and panicky wireless operators.

We crossed the French coast without incident and flew on across Northern France. Wireless reception was good, the broadcasts from control coming through loud and clear. This greatly eased the wireless operator's burden, for when reception was bad, or heavy interference was experienced, the worry of missing a broadcast added much to the strain of an operation. Should the group be diverted to another target, or recalled, and the message not recorded, the consequences could be serious.

We worked largely in silence and a passenger observing us might have been surprised by the routine and matter-of-fact way in which our various duties were carried out. From time to time the skipper would call up every crew member on the intercom just to make sure that no one had lost his oxygen supply or let his inter-communication socket become detached. The gunners, in their movable turrets, were always likely to pull out a socket when turning, no matter how long the lead might be. Apart from this, however, no one spoke unless he had something of importance to say.

Consequently, when I saw a contact appear on my visual monica screen I waited a moment to see whether it would pass off, before warning the captain and gunners. It remained very steady at about 400 feet; so after a moment or two I told Ernie. He asked if the gunners could see anything, but they could not. We then carried out an exercise to determine whether the other aircraft was above or below us. This consisted of rocking the aircraft by banking to port and then to starboard. As I have already explained, the aerial nearest to the contacted aircraft would record the stronger signal and this would show on the screen. Therefore, if we banked left and the port aerial recorded the stronger signal, the following aircraft was below. If on the other hand the starboard aerial recorded the stronger signal, it was above. By then banking to the right we could obtain a double check; a converse reaction confirming the previous conclusion.

This example I have given presupposes ideal circumstances: an aircraft dead astern. If the aircraft were not dead astern, however, it was more difficult to determine its position accurately for of course one aerial would already be recording a stronger signal. In these circumstances, a captain was dependent on the skill of his operator in interpreting the impulses.

The gunners knew that mistakes could easily be made and so were rightly inclined to trust their eyes rather than a radar box. On this occasion, the conditions were ideal for interpreting the impulses and I confidently asserted that this aircraft was below. Still the gunners could see nothing.

We flew on for a minute or two, the 'blip' remaining stationary at 400 feet. Then suddenly, and dramatically, my worst fears were confirmed: the 'blip' shot to the bottom of the screen, and before I could switch on my microphone cannon shell pounded the belly of 'Able'.

'Jesus, I got it.' It was Joe's voice. Turning round towards him I saw the armour-plated door behind me had been shattered and there a few yards away sat Joe, slumped in his turret, and beneath him the flare chute was burning. In a moment the entire fuselage was alight. Flames licked up through the floor as the incendiaries burned in the bomb bay. They spread to the walls, then the roof. In a matter of seconds the aircraft was an inferno. 'Jettison the bomb load,' someone shouted; 'get rid of the cookie.' The 'cookie' was a 4,000-lb bomb and these incendiaries were blazing round it. Ernie shouted something about the bomb bay doors not opening. I grabbed a fire extinguisher and so did Harry, but it was hopeless. 'Abandon aircraft! Jump, jump!' It was Ernie's voice, and for a moment I had a mind to question the order. So quickly had this decision been brought about that my mind was hardly equal to the situation. 'Bomb-aimer jumping', 'Navigator jumping', 'Engineer jumping', 'Wireless operator jumping'. I grabbed my chute and clipped it on. 'Gunners, gunners,' Ernie was shouting, but no answer came. An icy blast whipped down the fuselage from the nose, telling us the escape hatch was away and simultaneously urging the flames behind me to greater vehemence.

I pulled off my helmet and moved towards the hatch. At that precise moment the nose went down with a suddenness that lifted me off my feet and threw me towards the flames. Then we straightened, and the force of G knocked me to my knees. I felt as if the elements were playing cat and mouse, and my mind, tortured by awful reality, brought every muscle, nerve and sinew to bear and allowed me to drag myself towards the kinder, colder world outside the escape hatch.

A shapeless figure dived out in front of me, hitting the side of the hatch on the way. Even in my terror I took heed of what I'd seen and dived out as compactly as possible.

A great blanket of air hit me hard and appeared to rush me up towards the heavens. I waited some moments before pulling the ripcord, and then have no recollection of what happened till presently I found myself suspended in space, apparently ascending rapidly. For some moments – I know not how long – strange thoughts passed through my mind. Was I dead? If not, what had happened to me? Was I climbing towards the stars? How did I get here? Where had I come from?

The events of only a few seconds before had been forgotten utterly and completely, and a puzzled brain strove desperately to understand where it was, and why. Whilst body and brain wrestled with this problem, I, apparently detached from myself, watched with interest this struggle in search of reason. I can offer no explanation of this experience. It may have been due to lack of oxygen – we had jumped at high altitude – or it may have been a spiritual experience. I don't know. But whatever it was, it could not have lasted for long, for soon I was one again, swinging backwards and forwards with the mixed feelings that only those who have made an emergency jump can understand and appreciate: the thankfulness that one has saved one's life is tempered with the realization that what has just passed has been awful. My mouth was dry, my heart was pounding, the air was terribly cold. I made to put my hands in my pockets and found that I was still holding the ripcord handle – a metal affair. When my hand released its hold, it remained frozen to the palm. A shake, and it was away, accompanied by a good portion of skin. For a moment the pain was intense, but it dulled once the hand was in my pocket. Above me the air whistled through the hole in the centre of my 'chute, telling me that I was falling quite fast. I peered into the inky blackness that was everywhere, but saw nothing. Then without warning, a great flash appeared, followed immediately by an explosion. A blast of air took my parachute and spun me round and round so that my straps became entangled and I feared the 'chute would collapse. My hands shot up, and I blessed the comprehensiveness of our training, for I soon righted myself. Beneath me a hundred fires burned, lighting the surrounding countryside, which, thick with snow, at once reflected all the light. And there lay all that remained of 'Able' and perhaps ...

The 4,000-pounder had spread a blanket of incendiaries over a wide area and it was now possible to appreciate how fast I was falling. Not only was I dropping, I was drifting so quickly that in a minute or two the fires were too far away to help me any more. When they suddenly disappeared, leaving only a glow in the sky, it was obvious that the ground was near, for something was between the fires and myself – a wood, as it happened – and I prepared to land.

What really saved my limbs, however, was a dog, which barked furiously – probably hearing my parachute – and bracing myself I made violent contact with ground and netting.

My surprise at the hardness of the ground was exceeded by the indignation of those who had been peacefully slumbering beneath the netting. The arrival of an additional bedmate was not appreciated, and whilst both they and I struggled to emerge from under the parachute,

their overtures were deafening and unmusical. I had
landed in a chicken-run.

Once free from the encumbrance of the parachute, my
new acquaintances scattered in all directions. Freedom, if
only temporary, was theirs, yet they faced it – or so it
seemed – with as much misgiving as I now viewed my
prospective capture.

For some little time I sat there, too stunned to move,
expecting any minute to hear guttural German voices, and
wondering whether someone would run a bayonet
through me, or if an angry mob would drag me to the
nearest lamppost.

The landing had been severe. My legs and back ached
dreadfully, and the blood from a small wound in my neck
ran down to form a puddle in the hollow between my
collar-bone and shoulder-blade. I moved, and it passed on
down my chest like warm water from a sponge. So far as I
could see, the chicken-run was in a small field, surrounded
by a wooden fence. Behind this fence there appeared to be
the outline of buildings, but I could not be sure. Not a
sound could be heard. The night was cold, dark and still.
My feathered friends had gone and now rested noiselessly
somewhere out in the darkness. I wondered what had
happened to the dog who had barked so fortunately. What
had become of him?

And the people in those houses, they must have heard
the chickens herald my arrival? An uncanny feeling grew
over me. It was as if I were sitting in a city of the dead.
Then, as I peered out into the darkness, there came a just
perceptible sound. I strained still harder and made out a
small figure standing a little beyond the fence. For a
moment or two neither of us moved. Then, reasoning that
if he were going to raise an alarm he would already have
done so, I got to my feet and went warily towards him. The
figure never moved but demanded in high-pitched voice,
'Etez-vous anglais ou amèrican?' It was a little boy.

'Je suis anglais,' I answered; 'êtes-vous mon ami?'

He held out a little hand; I took it.

'Pouvez-vous m'aider?' I asked.

'Attendez un moment,' he replied and disappeared in
the darkness. In a few moments he was back again with

three young lads whom he introduced as his brothers. They shook me warmly by the hand and at my suggestion one of them ran off to hide the parachute. More people emerged from the darkness. Every woman kissed me, every man gripped my hand, but no one made any attempt to help me. While I was relieved to find myself among friends, and greatly appreciative of the sincerity of their welcome, my desire to disappear before any Germans arrived was very strong. My new friends were apparently more interested in me as a curio from the sky rather than as an airman trying to evade capture and continued to chatter away, while I became more agitated as each minute passed.

Finally, when their conversation centred on my fur-lined flying boots, I felt compelled to ask if anyone could help me. My question stopped all conversation and we stood in silence.

Then a thickset figure thrust himself through the crowd, shook my hand, and bade me follow him. The crowd were as pleased as myself, and as I moved through them the women murmured in frightened relief. My rescuer moved rapidly, and I followed, feeling like a drowning man who has found a straw that will support him. He led me out of the field, into a cobbled road and down a little hill. There was silence, save for the sound of his steel studs on the stones, and the darkness was only pierced by sparks of light that flashed from his heels.

We soon arrived at a house. He opened the door and bade me enter. I found myself in a kitchen, farmhouse style, with a long black range, barred wooden shutters and a flagstone floor.

Three rather frightened-looking women stood there eyeing us apprehensively. My rescuer, speaking too rapidly for me to follow, explained my presence.

I saw now that he was in late middle age, thickset and strong, with greying hair and pale blue eyes which gazed sadly over a large bushy moustache. To anyone who, like myself, had lived in France, he was the exemplification of the peasant farmer

The eldest of the women, a short, middle-aged, kindly-faced soul, limped up and embraced me. She was a cripple with some deformity of the hip. He regarded this display of affection with approval and beckoned to the others, who followed suit. The crippled woman was his wife, the others daughters. Two chairs were then placed in front of the range. He bade me sit in one and took the other, the women remaining standing. He eyed me critically for some moments, as he might have studied a horse prior to purchase, then snapped out an order, simultaneously raising a hand to my chin and turning my head to get a better view of the wound in my neck. His daughters staggered up and placed a large round tub in front of the range which they immediately began to fill with hot water from a black cauldron simmering near the fire. Cold water was added, until their mother, testing it with a bared elbow, approved the temperature. I was then invited to bathe, and having no alternative but to accept, undressed and got into the water, whilst they watched with great interest.

There are few things more stimulating than a hot bath. As well as removing the clotted and congealed blood that was about me, the warm water put new life into limbs that had been both bruised and frozen. My rescuer talked briskly and I did my best to follow the gist of what he said. There were no Germans in the vicinity, I gathered, but they would naturally come to look for any airmen who might have baled out of the plane which had crashed.

'How far away was the crash?'

He was not sure. Everyone had heard the explosion and seen the fires, but it was several kilometres from Lor and we would have to wait till the morning for more news.

'Lor!' Was 'Lor' the name of the village? 'Of course!' They all laughed as if it were incredible that anyone should not know such an obvious thing.

'Where was the nearest town?'

'Rheims.' We were thirty kilometres north of the great cathedral city.

What could he do to help me?

Ah! Well! He could give me civilian clothes and hide me for three or four days until things had quietened down. Then – here he tapped his nose knowingly and winked – he would contact friends, who would come, perhaps in a car – he raised his eyebrows at the mention of the word 'car', and waited for me to make a suitable exclamation of surprise – and take me away. After that, who knows? He waved his hands expansively: 'Spain, Switzerland, the English Channel.' It all sounded so very easy. I imagined myself home again, leaning against the mess bar, surrounded by an inquiring crowd, modestly giving an account of my adventures. I saw myself on leave in Richmond, walking down the towpath with a girlfriend, enjoying a well-earned rest after my vicissitudes on the Continent. Then I saw myself captured and a prisoner of war, and the farmer, his wife and his daughters standing before a firing-squad. Yes, for me there was hope of escape and chance of capture, failure meant a boring detention till the cessation of hostilities. For them there was only one chance, the chance of being caught and its consequences: the torture chamber and final execution. Why should they do this for me? Why? ... but my host was speaking, asking me a question.

'The invasion, what about the invasion?'

'It will be soon,' I said.

'When?'

'I do not know, but soon.'

He nodded and, handing me a towel, picked up my uniform and flying boots and left the room.

I dried myself as discreetly as one could before three staring women and put on my flying underwear, all that now remained of my clothes. With remarkable speed the bath was whipped away and a table took its place. The farmer returned with some blue overalls and a pair of old boots. The overalls were too small, not reaching much below my knees. The boots were far too big, and even with thick flying socks on were loose enough to come off should I have to run. I felt ridiculous and ill at ease.

His wife dressed my small neck wound and dabbed iodine on my palm, which, minus skin, had suffered from a surfeit of hand-shaking.

A plate, knife and fork were put on the table, a frying-pan appeared, and in no time at all two eggs were placed in front of me. At no time in my life had I felt less like eating, but what could one do? No bread was offered with the eggs, and knowing how short of food these people were I did not ask for any.

While I was eating my host left us yet again, to return a few minutes later with a bottle of champagne. He walked dramatically towards me and for a moment I was alarmed, thinking he had bad news, but it was only his characteristically French way of dramatizing an incident.

'My friend,' he said with great feeling, 'my friend, when the Germans came, they took all my wine, all my champagne. I hid but one bottle; this is it.' He paused to let the significance of his words sink in.

'I vowed then that I would open it only when the first Englishman landed in France. You,' and his voice trembled with emotion, 'are the first.'

Never in all my life had I felt so foolish. In the first place, dozens of Britons had been falling on France, as I had done, ever since the bomber offensive began. In the second, standing there in those ridiculous overalls, in boots several sizes too big, with a large bandage covering a tiny wound in my neck, I felt anything but the Saviour of France. My protests were of no avail. The bottle was uncorked, and our glasses raised to his toast of 'Les Alliés'.

The atmosphere was so electric I half expected everyone to throw the glasses over their shoulders. Instead they downed the contents in a gulp and were ready for more. There was an uncomfortable pause for a moment until it became apparent they were waiting for me to empty my glass. The French peasant does not sip his wine, he drinks it, and makes no attempt to hide the fact that the experience is enjoyable. We, on the other hand, tend to take longer, and our refined little sips both amuse and astonish them. Etiquette demanded that my glass should be refilled first, and suddenly realizing this I drank, in what was meant to be the French manner, with great abandon. Unfortunately, as I was not French nor familiar with champagne, a little of it went the wrong way, and in trying not to choke I emitted a noise so strange that my host nearly dropped the bottle in surprise and the women recoiled as if expecting me to explode. What explanation I would have given I don't know, but my inventiveness was not taxed, for a heavy knocking on the back door distracted their attention sufficiently for me to regain my composure.

For a moment everyone feared the worst, but some indignant questioning produced the answer that the caller was Madame Leroux, the schoolmistress from La Mal Maison. The door was unbarred and a plump sad-faced woman entered. She was obviously a trusted friend and we were introduced immediately. To my surprise she spoke to me in English and, though her English was no better than my French, it was pleasant to leave the translating to someone else. She, the farmer and myself, shared the last of the champagne. Custom demanded this, so I knew better than to protest, though I felt sorry for the mother and daughters who could appreciate it so much more than myself.

Madame Leroux was a widow, her husband having been killed in the retreat of 1940. She had arrived in the village that evening and had heard about my arrival and place of hiding. This seemed rather alarming news, but they assured me that the person who had told Madame Leroux was to be trusted, and had only passed on this information because she knew Madame would help.

For some little while we discussed the possibilities of escape, Madame Leroux, like the farmer, being optimistic. They were fascinated by the handkerchief map I produced and by a button compass I had retained when the farmer took away my clothes. My champagne finished – it had been sipped this time – coffee of sorts was produced in big bowls like small pudding basins. A rectangular lump of sugar – rather like a piece of soda – was placed in the bowl and very black coffee was added almost to the point of overflow. Then, using a tablespoon, the sugar was ground against the bottom of the bowl till dissolved, and the coffee was drunk like soup from the spoon. Despite its peculiar taste, I enjoyed it.

I had not slept the previous night, having passed the time in a much-delayed train returning from leave. This fact, allied to the exhausting experiences of the evening, the champagne and the heat of the fire, produced a feeling of sleepiness that was overpowering. No soporific could have been more effective, and the coffee for all its strength did nothing to impair my desire for sleep. 'He is tired,' said Madame Leroux, seeing me stifle a yawn. The farmer agreed, and I was led upstairs and put to bed in an old four-poster.

As I lay there in the darkness, finding it hard to believe all that had happened and wondering whether escape was really possible, the first of our aircraft returning from Augsburg passed overhead. The droning of the engines went on for some twenty minutes; then there was silence. For them the night would soon be over, the debriefing, the bacon and eggs, the comments on those who had not returned and then sleep. One always slept well after an operation; too tired to use one's imagination, too far away to study one's handiwork. A solitary aircraft became audible and passed by flying much lower than the others. An engine misfired several times and was cut, the others revved still harder. A 'Lanc' flying on two engines, I thought, left behind and alone – hope he makes it. Then with the thought that his chances were considerably better than mine, I went to sleep.

Four

I awoke the next morning immediately aware of my situation. There are some who, after a taxing experience, awake wondering where they are, only to remember – all too suddenly – their predicament. Others, because of what has happened, find sleep impossible, and torment themselves throughout the night with pessimistic thoughts and morbid imagination, so that the morning finds them exhausted. In my case there was no insomnia, no shock on waking; merely an active awareness of all that had occurred. It was only when I tried to sit up that my body revealed the sting left behind by the happenings of the night before. There seemed to be bruises everywhere, and where there were no bruises, special kinds of aches and pains, as in my neck and right hand.

There was a knock on the door and in came Madame Leroux the sad face of the night before now creased with smiles.

'I have a surprise for you,' she said, 'a big surprise,' and in walked Harry Middleton. For a moment we stared at one another in astonishment.

'Where on earth have you come from?' I gasped, 'and what's happened to your shoulder?'

'It's broken,' he said in a matter-of-fact way. 'I broke it when baling out.'

'You must have jumped just in front of me,' I said. 'I saw someone hit the side.'

'It was probably me,' he answered. 'I first knew about it when the 'chute opened. It gave me merry hell on the way down.'

I winced at the mere thought of hanging in a parachute harness with a broken shoulder.

'What happened after you landed? How did you get here?'

He laughed.

'Well! My landing was ruddy hard and didn't do this shoulder any good; in fact I had one hell of a job to get the harness off. I knew I was in pretty poor shape and needed help, and that no one would find me sitting out there at the back of beyond; and it was too cold to wait till morning, so I started to walk. After a while I found a road and reckoned it must go somewhere, so I just kept on going. I had to stop and rest every now and then, but eventually I reached this place. I was all in and knocked on the first door I came to. That old boy's face was a picture; two of us in one night!'

He paused and pondered on the humour and coincidence of the situation for a moment, and then went on:

'He brought me in and everyone fussed around, all talking at once. I can't understand a word of the lingo, so it was double Dutch to me, but I suppose they were talking about you. I saw the time was three o'clock and that I'd got them all out of bed, but even so they gave me coffee and some food and fixed me up on a couch downstairs. I'd just dozed off, or so it seemed, when this lady,' he indicated Madame Leroux, who had been listening impassively, 'woke me up and said she had a surprise for me. I was so pleased she could speak English that I didn't think much about the surprise but followed her up here, to find you. What does it all mean? Can they really help us?'

'But of course,' interjected Madame Leroux. 'First, however, you must have a doctor. He will make you better. You must trust us to know what is best, and do what we tell you.'

We both nodded our assent, only too pleased that someone could tell us what to do.

Over a hurried breakfast I gave Harry a brief account of my own experiences since landing. We then parted, he to wait for the doctor, I to be hidden in a barn near the farm.

This barn housed a haystack which was made up of dozens of brick-shaped bales, about four feet square, and bound with corded straw rope to keep them compact.

They had been stacked one on top of the other until they filled the building from floor to roof. Probably with the idea of providing a hiding-place for himself, relatives or Maquis members, the farmer had arranged his stacking in such a way that a small chamber, rather like a priest's hole, was left in the middle of the barn. Access was known only to his family and himself. As he moved each bale, one here, one there, a veritable labyrinth was exposed leading ultimately to this tiny sanctuary. He gave me a blanket and a medicine bottle filled with what he called 'whisky', and shaking my hand left me to my own devices. As each bale was pushed back into position, both light and sound diminished, till the insulation of my burrow was complete.

The air was thick and musty with the smell of hay, and I hoped that sufficient for my needs would pass through the bales. For some time I sat expecting my eyes to pierce the darkness; soon, however, it was obvious that no light could reach me. My sojourn was to be a waking sleep.

The hours passed slowly. I had no watch, no means of knowing how long I must lie there with only my thoughts to comfort or mock me. To be entombed in this barn was to feel endowed with the imagination of an Edgar Allan Poe: suppose the farmer did not return? After all some catastrophe such as the discovery of Harry by the Germans would lead to the arrest and death of them all, save Harry, if he were still in uniform.

What would happen then? Would the Germans burn the farm as an example to others? I had heard of their doing this. If they did, my shouts would be of no avail, I would perish all too quickly – yet not quickly enough. Suppose no one came. How long must I wait before trying to find my way out? There is no sense of time after hours of darkness, no measure by which a man can assess duration.

After hours of forced and unaccustomed meditation, the mind boggles, and wanders aimlessly in the past. Scenes from childhood are recalled, incidents remembered, people and places pass in an unending flow, reminding one of other days, when Father Christmas was real and birthdays were days of magic. Such pleasant reveries cannot last for long, some incident from the past

calls up the present with a rush. I wondered how my
parents, grandparents and relatives would take the news;
whether my girlfriend of the moment would really care; if
my friends would be sorry. I answered none of these
questions, indeed I could not, any more than I could avoid
them.

There was a sound, an unmistakable sound. Someone
was coming. Gradually, as each bale was moved, light
found its way to my chamber, allowing my eyes to
accustom themselves to the visible world again. The last
bale moved and revealed the face of a youth unknown to
me. He did not enter, but held out his hand in greeting. I
roused myself and shook it, stifling a cry with difficulty
when his hard palm met the plaster on my skinless one. 'I
have brought you food,' he said, and handed me an
enormous sandwich, a long French loaf split down the
middle, spread with jam, and then folded again. I thanked
him and asked the time.

'Two o'clock,' he answered. 'You will come back to the
house at six. Your friend,' he went on, 'has seen the doctor
and is much better.'

I was pleased to hear Harry was well, but very distressed
at the thought of four further hours of dark solitude, so
resolved to keep the lad engaged in conversation for as
long as possible. 'Won't you come in and have a drink with
me?' I asked.

At the sight of the bottle of so-called whisky he showed
some interest and dropped down into my burrow. I
uncorked the bottle, and an aroma not unlike methylated
spirits wafted out and scented the musty air. After a mild
and affable dispute as to who should drink first, I bowed
to his wishes and took a tentative swig at the bottle. For a
moment it was as if my mouth was filled with hot coals.
Lights flashed before my eyes, and with a rush all breath
left my body. I gasped, coughed, leant back against the
bales and strove to fill my empty lungs. The youth gave a
cry of delight, and taking the bottle from my hand
rendered himself temporarily as incapable as myself. It
was some moments before either of us could speak. My
friend handed the bottle back to me, obviously determined
to enjoy the agony of a repeated performance. At first I

demurred, but the powerful alcohol was working fast, and under its influence I took another swig. So did he, and in no time the medicine bottle was empty, and he was sitting on the ground eating my sandwich without a care in the world. It was after three o'clock when he left, and before the last bale fell into position I was asleep. This home-made brew had done its stuff, and though my intestines might never be the same again I blessed the contents of that bottle.

I awoke cold and stiff to hear the sound of bales being moved, and soon the farmer was helping me out of my hiding-place. Apart from a headache I was none the worse for my solitary confinement but hungered for the warmth of a fire. We entered the kitchen of the night before and there was Harry in front of a veritable furnace. Whilst I gloried in its warmth, Harry recounted the happenings of the day. The doctor had worked quickly and silently. Neither by word nor by gesture had he intimated to Harry that he knew who he was. This had, of course, been deliberate policy. Various people came in and shook hands with us, and children played around the kitchen table.

'It's like Waterloo Station. How long it'll be before Jerry tumbles to what is going on I don't know,' Harry grumbled.

I agreed with him from the security point of view, though from a purely selfish angle it was pleasant to be with people again.

'It's not for myself or you,' he went on, 'but they'll all be shot if they find us here. We don't want that on our consciences.' One could only agree, yet we could not instruct them as to their own security.

A meal followed, and our host was affability itself. Neither of us had much appetite. I suppose we could have eaten really good food with relish, but the food was poor and, as yet, I was not hungry. The meal over, a small radio was produced, and the strains of 'Blaydon Races' filled the room. Harry swore in surprise, and then looked so dejected that I had to quickly explain that he was a Newcastle man, or 'Geordie', and that this was the song of his town – like 'Sur le Pont d'Avignon'. Everyone nodded understandingly. The news followed, and when the announcer gave details of aircraft losses for the previous night we felt like two men hearing a reading of their own obituaries. Madame Leroux came in later, and was very kind, but had no news for us, and the conversation passed to the most mundane things; questions about our homes, what we hoped to do after the war, and so on. They were all most inquisitive about the smallest details, and we did our best to satisfy their curiosity, though it was hard work. Madame Leroux did all the talking, translating for both sides. I found that my French was coming back to me all the time, and indeed I was following everything that was said. I decided to keep this fact to myself for the present, feeling they were more likely to discuss any difficulties in front of us if they believed we could not understand. Earlier, I referred to my conversations with the farmer and others. These were fairly lengthy affairs, for both of us were striving to make the other understand, and did not hesitate to add sign language to our vocabularies.

The time came for Madame Leroux to leave, and once she had gone everyone went to bed. Harry and I shared a downstairs room, sleeping on the floor on straw mattresses. We were asked to sleep fully clothed, and of course agreed. With only a couple of blankets between us I was none too warm, and sleep did not come easily. I dozed off eventually, only to be awakened from time to time by Harry, who groaned terribly. He had not complained all evening, but now in sleep acknowledged the aching of his broken limb. I respected his courage, and longed to help him, but there was nothing I could do. We were aroused at first light, and after a bowl of coffee in bed followed the farmer over the frozen countryside to a haystack about a quarter of a mile from his house. I carried a hayfork, as did one of the farmer's lads, and we all tried to look as casual as possible, though no one seemed to be about. The haystack was under a tin roof supported on iron girders, and it was up these girders we had to climb to reach the top, no easy feat for Harry with only one arm, even with the French lad below him and myself above. Once on top, we burrowed down into the hay both for warmth and security, but left a self-made peephole so that we could watch the farm and its environs. The farmer left some food and wine with us, and said they would return at nightfall. At first we entertained ourselves by watching the village come to life. These good people had, of course, risen as early or earlier than ourselves, but until they began to busy themselves outside the blackout hid them. There was little traffic on the road to entertain us, and after a while we tired of watching, and occupied ourselves in improving our hiding-place. It was bitterly cold, and Harry, restricted in his movements by his sling, suffered more than I did. We talked together to pass the time, going over the same thing again and again – was escape possible? We consulted our handkerchief maps, fiddled with our compasses, picked at our rations, sipped the wine, and at long last evening came, and with it our host. He had wisely brought along two young fellows to help him get Harry down to ground level, and he needed them badly. Apart from his arm, Harry was now very cold and stiff and could do little to help himself, but, my word! how he tried. Eventually we got him down, then went back to the farmhouse and that wonderful fire. Madame Leroux came again after supper, and this time had bits and pieces of news.

'Your navigator broke his leg, and the Germans have taken him prisoner. The people who found him would have helped him, but what could they do?' She shrugged her shoulders, and then went on:

'You had a Canadian friend?'

We nodded.

'I am sorry, but he is dead; he was badly wounded and died on his parachute.'

We questioned her as to where Joe had been found, and she insisted that he had made a parachute jump and had not been found anywhere near our aircraft. This puzzled us, for we were both sure poor Joe had died in 'Able', even before we had jumped. There was no news of Ernie or Tom, and we both feared the worst. Her news both saddened and depressed us, and our mood affected everyone. No repetition of the previous evening's optimism was possible and shortly after nine o'clock we went to bed.

The next day followed the pattern of the previous one: we rose early and went to our haystack. We had the same trouble getting Harry up there, and even more getting him down, and the day was as uneventful, tedious and cold as we had expected it to be. We were both beginning to feel that the strain of hiding us was affecting our helpers, they snapped at one another and looked worried and morose. When we questioned them about what was going to happen next, we were told that we must wait for their friends to come in a car. Something was wrong, we felt sure, and I went to bed with a feeling that no friends would come. Another thing that puzzled me was why no Germans had been in the area to look for us; something was certainly not quite right.

We slept upstairs that night, both in the same bed in which I had spent my first night. Why we were moved I don't know, but we thought it was because of some family dispute. We discussed the whole situation in bed and wondered whether we ought to press on by ourselves so as to relieve our friends of their dangerous responsibility. But where could we go with Harry injured as he was, though he was game for anything?

We were wakened the next morning by Madame Leroux, who burst into the room crying:

'The Germans know you are here; we have been betrayed.'

I leapt out of bed quite as frightened as when I'd baled out of 'Able', and asked for an explanation. She said someone in the village had told the Germans we were there, and the only way they felt they could save their lives was to hand us over as prisoners, saying we had surrendered to them and they in turn were passing us on.

'Don't run away,' she pleaded. 'Stay and be taken prisoner. They will not hurt you, but they may shoot us.'

We both allayed her fears.

'We'll stay all right,' said Harry, 'but you'd better let us have our uniforms back or it'll look queer.'

'The men are getting the uniforms now,' she answered. 'They were well hidden, but they will not be long.'

A man soon arrived with Harry's uniform and he changed, and for the first time dispensed with his sling.

He was pale and very ill, and seeing me looking at him said:

'I'd never have made it, anyway, but you might have done. I'm sorry.'

'Sorry for what?' I asked. 'It's not your fault.'

'Maybe not,' he said, but something was going through his mind, and after a minute's pause he added: 'Moving a fit chap is one thing, moving someone like me is another. When I turned up they had to change their plans. I'm sorry.'

'My God, they had no time to make plans! You were here an hour or two after me.' I tried to sound angry so as to make him feel he was being ridiculous, but he was ready to accept capture and the blame for it, as a matter of course.

Madame Leroux, who had left us, came back as agitated as ever.

'Your uniform, it is down a well, we cannot get it.'

In her excitement and anguish she spoke in French, and I answered her in the same language, asking what she meant. She then spoke in English and we became involved, for Harry, catching on quickly, questioned her vigorously, and with everyone shouting in French it was bedlam. Fortunately the farmer returned, and with a firm expletive to those present stopped all chatter. He then turned to me and speaking slowly and carefully said:

'Your uniform is lost down a well; we cannot get it. If you have no uniform the Germans will be suspicious and question everyone and it may be the end of us all. You must run away as you are and we will say you escaped after asking us to look after your friend. You must do it; it is the only way.'

I was flabbergasted, and although this was, in a sense, an incredible stroke of good fortune, the thought of just running away and leaving Harry was unthinkable.

'I can't do it,' I said. 'I can't just leave him to the Boche. He needs me, I must stay.' Although these words came out of my mouth, I knew in my heart of hearts that I would have to leave him; there was nothing else I could do. The lives of our helpers were of paramount importance, superseding all personal considerations. Yet I would be a hypocrite if I pretended that the chance of escape was not attractive; it is supremely easy to find self-justification for the thing one wants to do, and Harry's injury and incapacity lent themselves readily to a mind seeking – all too eagerly – any excuse for a course of action attractive to its aims, agreeable to its wants.

'You must go, and there is no time to lose, they will be here in a few minutes. They'll not hurt your friend, he is a prisoner of war, they still respect that. Hurry! Hurry!'

I turned to Harry, who whilst I had been arguing with the farmer had obtained a rapid appraisal of the situation from Madame Leroux. He was smiling, and though he still looked ill had an expression of great relief on his face.

'You've had it,' he laughed. 'Go on, beat it. The quicker you get away the better.'

'I can't leave you, Harry.' I tried to sound as if I meant it, and in a sense I did; for if there had been a chance for both of us, I would truly have stayed, but I knew my decision was inevitable. The price of dalliance was too high. Neither our friends nor ourselves could countenance indecisiveness: their lives were at stake as well as my conscience.

'You've got no choice, old son. It's nothing to do with you or me now; it's them. You've got to do the right thing by them. Anyway, I've had it. I've been thinking of throwing my hand in for a day or two, only I thought it would look bad after what they've done for us.'

Harry was a poor liar, and his story carried no conviction, but his bravery brought a lump to my throat, and for a moment I was at a loss for words. I turned towards the window and saw the farmer's wife crossing the yard as fast as a poor crippled limb would allow, carrying a small parcel which, on entering the room, she gave to me. It contained my iron rations, the rations all flying men carried on operations so that they might have something to sustain them in circumstances such as these. Since the box had contained chocolates I had given it to her for the children, and she had said she would keep it until one of them had a birthday. Now she produced it from its hiding-place and handed it over, insisting that it was necessary, and that I would have need of it in the next few days. I shoved it into the pocket of a thin overcoat that had been given to me, and pulling on a beret turned to Harry.

'I'm sorry it's turned out this way, Harry. I feel awful leaving you.'

He smiled. 'You always talked too much. Go on, get moving, take your chance while you've got a chance. I'll be all right.'

Then he added in an undertone as if not wanting our helpers to hear: 'Don't let the bastards catch you, and don't look so damned sentimental in front of these Frenchies; we're British, you know.'

The farmer, who had been talking to Madame Leroux, now handed me a piece of paper with the name of a Resistance member on it, the school-teacher of a village to the west of Lor.

'Go to this man, he will help you. Just say you are one of the airmen from Lor; he will understand.'

I nodded, and putting the paper in my pocket, turned and bade farewell to everyone – there must have been twenty people in the room. All the women were crying and by the time I reached the farmer they were making quite a lot of noise.

'Be quiet, be quiet,' he shouted. 'Has he not enough to worry him?'

The babble diminished to a few sniffs and sobs and he was able to indicate to me which way I should go.

'See the wood over there?' he said, pointing through the window. 'Make for that. The Germans will start looking for you soon, so move as far as you can today. When you reach the other side of the wood you will see a village; wait till dark, and then go to the school-house and do what I said. Do you understand?'

I nodded.

'Good, then go at once and good luck!'

I took Harry's hand and tried to speak, but no words came.

'It's easier for me than you,' he said. 'Make the most of your luck, and when you're home have one for me. Now go to it!'

He gave me a shove and, managing a 'God Bless you, Harry,' I stumbled out into an icy north-east wind and headed for the distant wood. When I had covered about thirty yards I turned and looked back. Harry was standing at the window watching. He gave me a thumbs-up sign with his good arm and smiled. With a wave of my hand I turned again towards the wood and freedom, wondering if I could face the problems ahead with half his courage.

My journey to the wood was both painful and exhausting: my over-sized boots kept coming off, and the snow was deep enough to make me take tiring high steps. When I arrived, I fell to the ground exhausted. I tried to pull myself together, but my feet were so cold and painful that further exertion seemed impossible. But the human frame is capable of much more than we realize. It needs a spur, however, something to urge it on to greater effort. And when that something is found, hidden reserves pour out their energies, and ordinary standards of personal strength and fatigue are surpassed.

As I sat there, miserably rubbing my frozen feet and cursing the weather, the sound of a car being driven at high speed awakened me to the fact that I had put little distance between the farmhouse and myself. The realization that this heralded the arrival of Harry's captors made my heart pound and brought me to my feet, gazing back to the farmhouse. The car stopped, and three men got out and looked about them as if not sure where to go. The farmer appeared and beckoned, and they went into the farmhouse. I watched apprehensively, to see how they would emerge with Harry. Then, as I looked down across the snowy waste, smooth and white, a jagged scar appeared, stretching all the way from the main road to the edge of the wood at my feet, as if pointing me out as 'the one that got away'. I had left a trail pinpointing the exact spot at which I had entered the wood. Even at this moment the farmer would be saying how a young airman had asked them to look after his friend and then run away, and the German officer would walk to the window and see, as surely as if I had left a visiting card, exactly where the airman had gone. He would then go to the telephone, and within an hour troops would be here. Yes, there was a telephone in Lor, Madame Leroux had mentioned it, but it would take troops an hour to arrive, for the nearest were at Rheims, thirty kilometres away, the farmer had told me.

'I have one hour.' I turned and ran. I ran like a frightened rabbit. My boots came off. I stopped, picked them up and ran in my stockinged feet. The wood was thick so that the ground had only a moderate covering of snow and rapid progress was possible. Tall trees, thick trees, all loomed up in front of me like phantoms barring my path, but I was inspired by fear. I side-stepped, dodged and ducked with all the skill of a flying three-quarter making for the line, until a hand in the form of an offending root stretched out and catching my ankle sent me crashing to the ground. For a moment I lay stunned, blood flowing from my nose, my bruised and bleeding feet aching with an intensity I could barely endure. I got to my knees and prayed as only saints and frightened men can pray, and then went on. 'The Lord helps those who help themselves.'

Then in the distance I heard a hound baying. The effect was electric and finding further energy my tired limbs propelled me on at even greater speed. For something like an hour I kept moving westward, wondering all the while why the promised village did not appear. Sometimes I would be in open country, only too aware of how conspicuous I was, but there would always be more trees ahead, and I would make for them. Indeed the whole countryside seemed to be dotted with small forests, but no sooner did I imagine myself deep in the heart of a leafless jungle, than the trees would thin and snowy fields have to be crossed before further shelter appeared. For my direction I was dependent on a pocket compass. However, since my navigation consisted merely of stopping and checking that my progress was westward, it was soon obvious that this rudimentary method had been too primitive for me to find the village. The farmer had said it was on the other side of the wood. Well, I had passed through several woods without sighting a dwelling of any kind, let alone a village. I must, unwittingly, have bypassed it. I stopped to take stock of my circumstances and to reconsider my position. Physically my feet were now in such bad condition that my only chance of evading capture lay in finding a hiding-place near by. Whilst on the move, with the sound of that hound in my ears, fear had sent me far and fast, but now that I had actually stopped my feet hurt intolerably.

The baying of the hound was no longer audible, so it seemed reasonable to assume that I had temporarily outdistanced my pursuers, but it was only too obvious that with all the trails I had left in virgin snow in the open country they must find me sooner or later. I took out the piece of paper with the name of the village and the schoolmaster and chewed it to pulp, then limped on, looking desperately for somewhere to hide. The wind rose a little and whistled its way through the bare branches. The trees swayed slightly and creaked and groaned in chorus as if to protest at such treatment; the powdered snow blew up, whirled round the trees as if in play, then packed itself against the trunks and rested there, and once again came the baying of a hound. I urged myself on and on, but – as if in a nightmare – my feet were of lead, growing heavier and heavier with every step. My nose started to bleed, my vision became blurred, I was losing consciousness – then suddenly I was falling.

Falls invariably end abruptly and the body instinctively braces itself for the impact which it knows must follow. My body was no exception, so it was all the more extraordinary to feel, not a sudden arresting of all movement, but a gradual slowing down. When I finally stopped, I was deep in a snowdrift. I struggled on to my back, more to allow myself to breathe than to discover where I was, but looking upwards saw that I lay in soft snow at the bottom of a narrow pit some ten or twelve feet deep, with perhaps three or four feet of snow at the bottom. This had broken what might have been a nasty fall, but it had also – or so I thought – left me trapped to await my pursuers' pleasure. However, the tide of my resistance was at its ebb, and I passed into sweet unconsciousness. How long I rested there I do not know, but when I awoke it was dark and stars peeped at me through the branches overhead. The hound had failed to find me. I tried to sit up, and to my surprise managed it easily. I should have been frozen stiff, but wasn't. Standing up was a different matter, and though I got to my knees easily enough, the last stage was almost impossible, but self-exhortation and a frenzied desire to escape from this claustrophobic place saw me presently at the top, struggling to put on my boots. This done without much difficulty – my feet were too cold to hurt – I began to exercise as vigorously as possible, in an attempt to restore something like full circulation. I felt an elation at being still at large, and believed that more than luck was on my side after all the happenings since I baled out of 'Able'. Temporarily my chief worry was whether my feet were frostbitten. If they were, using them would make them no worse, if not, exercise might save them. So I ambled off, staggering from tree to tree, with no real plan in mind, but a determination to keep moving at all cost. The wood began to thin, and in the distance I fancied I saw buildings and headed towards them, wondering whether I dared to go to a house and ask for help. The first shape proved to be a haystack, which – even in the dark – appeared to be familiar. I circled it a couple of times, puzzled by the similarity of its shape and general appearance to the one in which Harry and I had spent two days. The construction of the girders was the same, and in the end I felt obliged to climb to the top, just to satisfy myself that I was not back in Lor. Once on top it did not take me long to find my former hiding-place. In some extraordinary way I had – despite the compass – returned to my point of departure. Yet, I had been heading westward all the time – or so I thought. Greatly puzzled, I moved down into the hay for warmth, and pondered on the situation that now confronted me. The desire to rush to the farmhouse with its warm fire, hot coffee and affable host was irresistible but quite impracticable: for all I knew the Germans might still be there, or at any rate near by.

Finally, I reasoned that the best thing to do was to spend the night where I was, then to watch the farmhouse and village during the following day, and if all appeared well to seek help after dark. This decision taken, and appreciating that it would be some twenty-four hours before I left the haystack, I concerned myself with making my hiding-place as comfortable as possible. Creature comfort is important at the best of times, but when spending a night out of doors, in bitter cold and with potentially frostbitten feet, it is vital. I tunnelled down a little until the wind, passing between the roof and the top of the haystack, was no longer a problem. Then I packed hay into my pockets and inside my overalls, effectively padding my clothing and increasing its warmth. These exertions warmed me and for the first time since leaving Harry I was almost comfortable. Although I had not eaten anything for twenty-four hours I was not hungry and decided to wait until the morning before opening my rations. I dozed off eventually, only to be awakened by a large barn owl, which flew under the roof and settled a few yards away on a steel rafter a little above my head and stared hard at me with large hypnotic eyes, as if to say: 'What the blazes are you doing here?' I was quite terrified lest he should attack, for he was very large, and his beak could have caused damage, but fortunately he was an amiable owl, and after staring me out several times, and cogitating for a while, he flew off and left me in peace.

The rest of the night was uneventful but, with only intermittent sleep, dreadfully long. When the dawn came, and all the cocks started crowing, I came up to the top of my burrow and watched anxiously to see whether all was well with my friends. I was soon reassured, for presently the farmer appeared, then his wife, and after a while the children, all shouting and laughing without a care in the world. Much relieved, I settled down to have breakfast, but found my hands were so swollen that, try though I would, I could not open my iron rations. They were sealed in a perspex container, and I simply could not break the seal. For thirty-six hours hunger had been no problem, but it was now. The perspex, being transparent, allowed me to see the bars of chocolate and other suddenly delectable offerings. I hit the container against a girder, but this was noisy so I had to stop. I tried stamping on it, but with hay as a foundation that was useless. Nothing I could do would open it, so I didn't eat!

Remarkably little happened in the village that day so far as I was concerned. I preserved my morale – or what was left of it – by counting all the windows I could see; then the chimneys, those that were smoking, those that were not;

and so on and so on – anything to keep my mind occupied. When the light began to go, it took all my will-power to stop myself from rushing to the farmhouse. I waited, however, and when it was really dark climbed down and moved warily to the house. Youthful voices were coming from one of the big sheds, so I crept up and peered through the door to see what they were up to, hoping to ask one of them if it would be safe for me to enter the house. There I saw some seven or eight children, sitting in a circle, talking and laughing happily, every one of them seated on a chamber. I entered and was greeted with cries of delight. The eldest boy, a lad of about ten, addressed me so politely that I half expected him to ask me to pull up a pot and sit down. After hearing that I wished to see his grandfather, and sensing the urgency of the situation, he roused himself and went into the house. A moment later his grandfather was embracing me as a long-lost son, and I was seated in front of the fire with food and drink before me.

Two fried eggs, black bread and a bowl of coffee were a feast; the warmth of the fire a sweet charity. I learnt that the Germans had treated Harry sympathetically, and had accepted the farmer's story without question. Some soldiers had gone out with a dog to look for me, but not being able to give the dog a scent they could only seek trails in the snow.

'They arrived very soon after you left,' said the farmer. 'I was afraid they might catch you when I saw them follow your trail, but you foxed them, eh!' He tweaked his nose and winked, whilst I shook my shoulders, too ashamed to try to explain my incredible good fortune. They listened open-mouthed to my account of what had occurred since I'd left them. I kept the story short, pretending the Germans had merely missed me in the wood, and saying nothing of my injured feet, for I did not want to stay with them, exposing everyone to danger for a second time. I hoped to rest for perhaps a day, and then try to make for the Swiss frontier. My plan was a vague one for, in fact, my last few hours in the haystack had been spent in contemplating the food and warmth I was now enjoying. When one feels that a situation is desperate, all horizons narrow, and first things come first. Self-preservation is the strongest instinct we have, but it is not to say that one must necessarily be selfish about it.

I felt ashamed at returning to the farmhouse at all, but I had tried to make sure it was safe for me to do so. All I expected was food, and perhaps a night's shelter, and to be on my way. I knew my feet would be a problem, but hoped they were merely bruised, and not frostbitten, and that rest and warmth would restore them. The fact that they had gone on supporting me, painful though they were, suggested that a tougher customer than myself would regard them merely as a hindrance, and not necessarily incapacitating. If I could only recover my fur-lined boots and Irving jacket, I felt that the weather could be faced with some prospect of success. My present boots and clothing were hopelessly inadequate, and only the fact that I had been very fit indeed before being shot down had seen me through that dreadful yesterday. How to bring up the subject without hurting their feelings was the problem.

The meal was no sooner over than Madame Leroux arrived, and my story had to be told again. She listened intently, and when I had finished said:

'You will have to come with me; it is too dangerous to stay here. Can you ride a bicycle?'

I nodded.

'Good! We will have to wait until later when the roads will be deserted, and then cycle to my lodgings in La Mal Maison. I have friends who will look after you.'

'But, madame,' I protested, 'it is too dangerous for anyone to travel with me on the road. If we were stopped …'

'We will not be stopped,' she insisted. 'The Germans have more to do than look for every airman who is shot down. They did not find you at once, now you are forgotten. There are too many of you. France is full of airmen.'

Feeling properly told off I did not argue any further, but sheepishly listened to and obeyed all further instructions.

We were to cycle without lights – a gesture to the curfew – and to take to the fields if stopped or surprised.

A little later I said goodbye to my friends for the second time, and accepting a proffered bicycle followed Madame Leroux up the road to La Mal Maison. I still had on the same thin clothing, but noticing the state of my hands and appreciating how cold one can become on a bicycle without gloves, the farmer had given me a pair of woollen ones. I had made inquiries about my flying boots and Irving jacket, but had been told, as before, that they were still down a well.

Madame Leroux cycled at a great pace and I was hard put to to keep up with her, particularly since she knew the road so well and I did not. We had only one bit of excitement, having to take our bicycles into a field and hide behind a hedge to let a car pass. Fortunately we had plenty of time, for with no traffic on the road an approaching vehicle could be heard when still a long way off. My feet stood up to the journey remarkably well, and I really began to believe that they were no more than badly cut and bruised.

Once we neared the outskirts of this little town – or big village – we dismounted, and walked quietly and cautiously through the deserted, snow-covered streets, until arriving at a small house. Madame Leroux signalled to me to stay where I was and went into the house. I heard muffled whispers, and then presently she reappeared and bade me enter. We passed through an old-fashioned porch into a small hall, where we left the bicycles, and then into a furnished sitting-room.

The light of the room was dazzling after the darkness and I blinked painfully at two rather apprehensive women who stood looking at me almost with awe. One of them was in her early twenties, the other perhaps the late thirties. Madame Leroux introduced them as friends of hers in the teaching profession who would be pleased to help me. I felt instinctively that Madame's personality had as much to do with their acceptance of this task as any patriotic motives, though to give them credit they did everything they could to make me comfortable. There was food and wine and the inevitable bowl of coffee and we spent a long time discussing recent happenings, possible future happenings and, of course, the invasion.

Eventually, when all of us were beginning to show signs of sleepiness, Madame suggested that the time had come to go to bed, and I learnt to my surprise that all of us were going to spend the night in this one small room. Why this was necessary I don't know, for Madame's colleagues had not known she was going to return with an evading airman, and so presumably were only visiting, and would have returned to their own quarters to sleep. Still, it was none of my business where they slept, so naturally I said nothing, but eyed the solitary double bed which filled a quarter of the room apprehensively. 'Monsieur must sleep in the bed,' said Madame. 'After two days and a night in the open he needs comfort, but we must be practical, the bed is big enough for two people at each end so we will sleep that way.' Then addressing me she said apologetically: 'I must put the stove out, we do not have enough fuel to let it burn all night. Since it will be very cold we must be sensible and share the bed. I know it is unconventional, but this is war.'

If sharing a bed with three women could be justified on the grounds that I was a combatant, it was little wonder that history was punctuated with wars. I offered to sleep on the floor myself, assuring them that after my recent experiences it would be luxury, but they would not hear of it, so I did as I was told and climbed into bed. To my surprise the youngest of these ladies jumped in beside me and began arranging the blankets in a very unconcerned way. There was a short eerie silence and then Madame spoke:

'Annette! I think it would be better if you slept at this end of the bed.' Annette demurred slightly and remained beside me. 'Annette!' Madame spoke again. She only said 'Annette', indeed it was all she had to say, for the tone of her voice demanded obedience. Annette muttered something under her breath and moved to the foot of the bed. Madame climbed in beside me, and after inquiring if everyone was comfortable, turned out the light.

The bed was wonderfully soft and with four fully-clothed occupants very warm. We had – under Madame's instructions – arranged things so that we lay in the most comfortable positions for alternate head, feet, head feet sleeping, but it was disconcerting to have a foot near one's nose if your opposite number happened to straighten a leg. In practice this would happen only if the owner of the foot were asleep, for it was prudent to keep your feet under cover. Still the possibility existed and I lay with a cupped hand between my chin and the foot nearest to it. After perhaps half an hour one of my feet began to ache terribly, and it was some time before I realised that Annette was tickling it. I moved it away, for it was too tender to bear even the softest caress; but, thinking no doubt that I wanted to play hard to get, Annette pursued it, till presently I was wriggling like an eel to escape her painful overtures. Everyone woke up of course, and there followed an uncomfortable period of silence and wakefulness during which I felt sure Madame longed to speak, but not being quite sure what had wakened her felt it more discreet to remain silent. Eventually they fell asleep again.

The following morning we rose early, and after the usual bowl of coffee Madame Leroux went out to make contact with the French Resistance, saying that she would return with good news. She impressed upon me that there were other people renting rooms in the building. We must be careful to speak in a whisper, and to keep away from the window, where the curtains had to be drawn so as not to arouse suspicion. Annette was to stay with me; the other teacher had to leave, to look after the school until Madame and Annette could resume their duties. At first Annette busied herself tidying the room while I stayed in bed, out of sight if not out of mind. I was a little concerned as to her intentions, for if a nod is really as good as a wink, I had – or so I thought – a good idea of what she was thinking. My apprehension was not due to any aversion to her, it was just that I felt ill and frightened. Her work finished, she came and sat on the bed near to me and smiled.

'There are no young men left in France,' she said. 'They are all prisoners of war or conscripted workers. This makes life very dull for the girls.'

'Of course,' I said, 'very dull.'

She moved a little closer.

'Have you a girl friend in England?'

I nodded.

'But of course you have! All you flying men are the same. I expect you have many of them.'

'One or two,' I said modestly, moving a little farther up the bed. She followed me, and pretending to avoid sitting on my legs sat very close to me, so that her face was only inches away from my own.

'Have you ever loved a French girl?' she asked, opening her mouth slightly and breathing rather heavily.

'No ... h' ... n' ... no,' I said, moving back nervously until my retreat was arrested by the top of the bed. 'No ... no, I have not known very many. When I lived in France I was very young. I did not think of such things.'

'Do you think of them now?' she asked, moving still closer, so that I was now pinned against the wall, her face, with its big blue inquiring eyes and twitching mouth, only inches away from my own. No powers of precognition were needed to see where all this was leading. I had to do something, if only to play for time, so I clasped her in my arms, moving my head so that my chin rested on her shoulder and I could stare out into the room. I found myself looking straight into a mirror on a chest of drawers in the far corner and saw the face of a wild young man with several days' growth of beard, longer near the point of the chin than anywhere else, giving him the appearance of a startled goat whose wild staring eyes cried out for help. His chin rested on the shoulder of a long-haired girl, her back curved in appreciation of the hands that clasped her. The young man held her tight for a moment or two, till suddenly she thrust herself away from him and the picture disappeared. It reappeared a few moments later, the face still wild, the eyes still staring, but with red lips tattooed on cheeks and forehead and a ruddy tinge to the beard. The hands clasped more tightly so that the next time the girl thrust, the face still remained in view, the knuckles whitening as they strove to maintain their hold. In vain the young man struggled. The face disappeared again, and did not reappear, for Fate intervened and rescued, or betrayed me. The caretaker of the building banged on the door, demanding to be let in to clean the room. A moment of panic followed, but fortunately

Annette was more than equal to the occasion once she had got over the initial shock, and indignantly told him that she was bathing, and that he would have to come back later. I thought this a pretty thin story, but learnt afterwards that the people in this part of the world had no bathrooms; they took a tub in whichever room was most convenient. He grumbled a bit, but accepted her story and wandered off.

For a while there was an uncomfortable silence, Annette standing looking out of the window, I sitting on the end of the bed. At last, unable to bear the tense atmosphere any longer, I spoke:

'Mademoiselle!'

She looked round.

'Mademoiselle! I hope you understand.'

'Yes,' she replied, 'I understand. It is your life, you must live it as you will.'

'I was not considering myself, mademoiselle.'

'Neither was I,' she replied.

After that there was not much else anyone could say, so I washed my face and got back into bed.

When Madame Leroux returned, she was accompanied by a young Frenchman, whom she introduced as a member of the Resistance. His youth and good looks rather belied Annette's tale that all the young Frenchmen were in Germany, though in fact, save for a few, her story was true.

He stayed only long enough to tell me that he would be returning after lunch with a friend who would take me to my next hiding-place.

'In daylight?' I asked.

'Why not? Indeed, it is safer.'

'Safer?'

'Yes, much safer, a car attracts too much attention at night.'

'A car!'

'Oh, yes. Silly of me not to mention it. You will be travelling by car.'

'But isn't that dangerous?'

'Of course, but not so dangerous as moving you on foot.'

'I thought only doctors were allowed cars?'

He laughed. 'And collaborators.'

'Your friend is a collaborator?'

'So far as the Germans are concerned. He is the Mayor of a nearby village and is allowed to use his car on official business.'

'Like moving British airmen,' said Annette.

He smiled and walked across to the door. 'I'll bring a razor with me this afternoon. With that beard you look anything but official business.'

Madame closed the door behind him and was about to lock it when he knocked. She opened it.

'I don't suppose you have any cigarettes left?' he asked me inquiringly.

'I don't smoke. I'm sorry.'

'So am I. Still, it can't be helped. See you this afternoon.'

Madame closed the door again and locked it.

'These young people are all the same. Cigarettes! I ask you!'

She busied herself with some papers, and it was a good hour before we sat down to a sparse picnic lunch; a bottle of wine, black bread and a rather evil-smelling salami-type sausage.

'Well,' said Madame, with an exaggerated cheerfulness she clearly did not feel, 'what have you two been doing this morning?'

'Oh, nothing in particular. I tried to entertain Monsieur, but with what success I don't know.'

She looked at me, her expressionless face revealing nothing.

'With great success, Mademoiselle. You were very kind.'

Madame nodded approvingly. 'Did anyone call?'

'Only the cleaner. I told him I was bathing and he went away.'

'But he will be back later. We must be careful or he will become suspicious.' Madame looked rather worried and turning to me added: 'In a village like this where everyone knows everyone else's business, it makes this sort of work very difficult. The old man has only to suggest that Annette would not let him into the room for everyone to presume she has a lover.'

'Oh, madame!' interjected Annette, 'what a thing to say in

front of Monsieur. You embarrass me.'

'Monsieur understands what I mean, don't you, monsieur?'

'Of course, madame. The same thing applies in an English village.'

Madame nodded. 'People always presume the worst and often they are quite wrong.'

'Did you hear that, monsieur?' Annette spoke pointedly but not without humour.

'What is the significance of that remark, Annette?' asked Madame.

'Significance, madame? Oh, it is just that you usually speak to Monsieur in English; I wanted to be sure that he understood your comment.' Madame looked at me apologetically. 'Forgive me, your French has improved so much during the last few days I forgot to speak slowly. Tell me, did you understand all I said?'

'Nearly all, madame.'

'This is splendid. In a short while you will speak like a Frenchman.'

'And perhaps behave like one,' added Annette.

Madame regarded her suspiciously. 'Annette, your remarks are confusing Monsieur, indeed I don't understand them myself; please be more explicit.'

Before Annette could answer, the sound of a car drawing up outside sent Madame to the window.

'They are here,' she exclaimed joyously, and waving me into a corner of the room opened the door. Our young friend of the morning and a man of about forty-five entered. The latter was introduced to me as the Mayor of Amifontaine, a large village some five kilometres away. Why the young man gave me this information I don't know; it would clearly have been more prudent not to reveal the man's precise identity, though he did not appear to mind.

He was a fairly tall thin man with sharp features and inquiring eyes. Indeed, so inquiring were these eyes that they gave his face a strange, quizzical expression. We shook hands and seeing me wince he asked for an explanation. I showed him my hand and he grimaced understandingly. 'You don't look too well, monsieur. I'm told you had a night in the open after a bad day on the run.'

Not wanting to discuss my minor injuries I pretended not to understand.

'I thought you said he spoke French!' He turned to the young man.

'He spoke very well this morning.'

'Oh, he speaks quite well but cannot follow you if you speak too quickly!' said Madame.

He nodded. 'Tell me about him.'

Madame ran quickly through the happenings of the last few days as she understood them, culminating with my arrival in this room the night before.

'He slept here?'

'Yes.'

'Where?'

'In the bed.'

'Not very gallant taking your bed.'

'Oh no, we all shared the bed,' Annette interjected.

His naturally curious expression became accentuated.

'All of you?'

Annette explained. He looked at the young man, then at me.

'Are you sure you want to leave, monsieur?'

'Of course.'

'Well, I'm afraid we cannot offer you such interesting sleeping arrangements elsewhere.'

'Monsieur le Maire!' Madame Leroux declared in shocked tones. 'How can you speak like that? This is no laughing matter.'

'Indeed, no, forgive me, but you must admit it's an incredible story, eh, Annette?'

Annette grinned wickedly, much to Madame's annoyance, and partly because of it.

'Perhaps Monsieur had better shave,' said Madame, changing the subject. 'It is not a good thing for your car to be seen outside here for too long.'

The Mayor agreed and the young man produced a cut-throat razor and a bar of soap. The razor was blunt and the soap refused to lather, so my efforts to remove about an inch of soft curly hair from my chin held their attention to the exclusion of all else. The hair on the side of my face gave me little trouble, but my luxuriant goatee beard was a different matter. Try though I would I could not scrape it off by any known method. I would rest the razor gently on my chin, then scrape upwards, then downwards, in the approved manner, but as if playing to the gallery the hair would curl away from the razor and fix itself to the clear parts of my cheeks as the non-lathering soap dried. In no time my face was very sore, and I very bad tempered. I decided to try another method, so washed the soap out of my beard, and took hold of the end of it and tugged it away from my chin, at the same moment looking slightly upwards. My audience watched in rapt fascination. I then took the razor and holding it rather as a violinist holds his bow prepared to saw off my beard.

'What is he going to play?' asked the Mayor.

'It will be something sad,' said the young man. 'Look at his face!'

I paused, as a temperamental musician might pause, and they were silent. 'It will have to be a quick, bold stroke,' I thought. 'Get it over ... now!' Most of the beard came away, and once the long hairs had gone soap, water and the normal method of shaving removed the rest.

The Mayor said something I could not understand and they all laughed.

I smiled weakly but said nothing. My face felt as if it had just come out of a bed of nettles, and a remark by Madame that I looked more like my old self did not seem complimentary.

'He is much younger that I thought he was,' said Annette. 'That explains a great deal.'

'There you go again.' Madame Leroux put her hands on her hips and regarded her junior with a look of puzzled bewilderment. 'What is the matter with you today? These inane remarks are most irritating.'

Annette, who was not one to be unduly bothered by an imbroglio no matter how complicated, smiled sweetly.

'Oh, madame, it is just that Monsieur and I were discussing his previous visits to France this morning. Some of the things he said seemed strange to me because I thought he was older than he is. Now I understand.'

'You women are all the same,' said the young man. 'A man is alone with you for a few hours and you know the story of his life.'

'Yes,' said the Mayor, intervening, 'they search our souls and discover everything about us, but we never know anything about them. Perhaps,' he added reflectively, 'it is just as well. When Eve made Adam curious he was banished from the Garden of Eden; it never pays to try to understand a woman. Enjoy their company; accept their favours; cherish their memory; but do not try to understand them, only God can do that.'

We laughed, and on this happy note said our goodbyes. Both Madame Leroux and Annette embraced me most affectionately and a tearful parting was only prevented by the Mayor, who told them they might not see him for a week, and he consequently expected similar treatment. To cries of 'We will tell your wife,' he ran out in mock alarm and started the car. Almost immediately the young man beckoned me to follow, and managing only a quick, 'Thank you for everything, madame; thank you, Annette,' I too ran out, jumped into the back of the car and was driven at great speed down the main street and out of the town.

My first impression was that the Mayor had gone berserk. With snow on the roads to drive at such speed was madness, particularly when, so far as I could see, there was no immediate hurry. Nor was speed enough for his insatiable temperament. He hooted ostentatiously at all and sundry and indeed appeared to do everything possible to attract attention. His design was to behave as normal. I was not to know it, but he always drove in this manner. The road was narrow, and like many French roads, steeply cambered from the centre to the side. We were continually sliding off the crown towards the ditch, returning to the middle as the Mayor skilfully corrected the drift. There was no doubt about it, he could drive a car. Still, my desire for a more conservative progress made me close my eyes, and I sat hoping we had not very far to go. Suddenly, after a particularly inspired period of revving in an intermediate gear, the engine stopped and we slithered to a standstill, fortunately – thanks to his skill

– still on the road. The other two leaped out and opened the bonnet, leaving me sitting in the back hoping that the Mayor's mechanical skill was equal to the verve and aplomb of his driving.

As it happened, it was, and we were soon on our way again, the two of them hooting with laughter at the apprehension on my face.

At last we reached our destination, a cottage on the outskirts of a village. It looked dilapidated and I felt a dislike for it which was to grow from day to day. We were welcomed by a tall, heavily built, rather untidy woman, who gave me a manly handshake and led us into the house. The first thing I noticed was the poorness of the fittings compared even with the relatively humble furnishings usually encountered in a French peasant's home. The spotless cleanliness of the farmhouse at Lor was missing, and a chicken had to be chased out of the kitchen into a large back yard, where several dozen other birds strutted round their pens or stared stupidly through the surrounding netting at the world outside. The frozen ground interfered with their usual scraping and pecking and they were at a loss for something to do, or so it seemed to me. The scene was dismal, bleak and depressing.

'Well, madame! We are much indebted to you for your kindness. If you will look after our young friend for a few days I assure you the Resistance will not forget it.'

The mayor spoke in a formal, very different tone of voice from the one he had used previously, and I felt that now he had delivered me safely he was only too anxious to leave, but was nevertheless extending exaggerated courtesy to this woman in the hope of flattering her into reliable co-operation.

'Yes, Monsieur le Maire, I cannot wait for the day when we will deal with the collaborators. It will be another Bastille day in the history of France.'

As she spoke, she opened a cupboard and took out a bottle of red wine, gathered four glasses in one large hand and set them on a table in the middle of the room, simultaneously removing the cork from the bottle with her teeth. She poured the Mayor a glassful, slightly less for the young man and myself.

'You are not the first one I have hidden,' she said, handing me a glass. 'I had an airman here for three weeks. He was difficult and made a fuss about the food. I hope you will not be so particular.'

'I do not speak French very well, madame,' I said. I wanted to play for time, her aggressive manner and appearance having taken me by surprise.

'Do not speak very well, eh! Well, you know some French, anyway. The last one knew nothing! Nothing! We could not make him understand a word, the fool.'

'And he could not make you understand a word of English, madame?'

For a moment there was a deathly silence, and the Mayor, who was in the act of raising his glass in a toast, stopped half-way with his mouth open. I could not help it; the words had just come out. For a moment, she was unsure of herself; she had not the wit to recognize the sarcasm; yet sensed that a particular meaning might be put on my words if she could only interpret them.

Her hesitation saved the day, for the Mayor was too wily to let half a chance of putting things right pass.

'Ah, madame! He does not know exactly what you have said, and does not understand exactly what he has said, but his meaning is clear: he wishes to agree with you.'

Madame looked only half convinced, but the Mayor took her aside and said in an undertone:

'His French is very poor – we have found it difficult not to laugh, but he is doing his best; be patient with him.'

Madame accepted his explanation and we toasted one another affably.

'I do not suppose you will see me again,' said the Mayor, after we had emptied our glasses. 'Others will pass you down the line, but good luck, and come back after the war.'

We shook hands, and noting that Madame was speaking to our young friend he added: 'Remember, a quick tongue, like a hasty heart, can be dangerous. You need her help, so put up with her ways. It will not be for long. Good-bye.'

They ran out, jumped into the car, and on the echo of a crisp exhaust note were gone.

For some little time there was an uncomfortable silence, whilst I looked out of the window and Madame looked at me. At last, she spoke: 'Come! I will show you your hiding-place, and the rest of the house.'

I followed her through four sparsely furnished rooms and a kitchen. Two of these rooms were bedrooms, one the living-room, and the other a storeroom of sorts.

This room had clearly been used as a dumping-place for any article no longer required on the farm, but which Madame did not want to destroy or throw away. Old pots and pans, bits of fencing, dirty sacking, a trough, and a pile of grain or chicken food from which ran an enormous rat when we entered.

'Ah, dirty beast!' she cried, and grabbing a small shovel used for measuring the grain, pursued the animal round the room, until she had it trapped in a corner. There was little light in the room, for there was no window, only a small grille high upon the wall. Such illumination as there was came through the open door in which I was standing.

'Get out of the light,' she cried. 'How can I see with you in the way?'

I stepped back into the living-room. The terrified rat, seeing the open door, made a run for it, but Madame was too quick for it. Whack! went the shovel, whack, whack! An almost human scream rent the air as the rat died, but Madame went on hitting, hitting, hitting, till presently she shovelled the pulverized mess across the room, and in the light of the door ensured that every piece and particle was in position on the shovel, not hesitating to use her hands to pick portions which, having fallen into cracks in the stone floor, could not be gathered any other way. She emerged with the gory mess, grinning.

'My chickens love a rat. Come and watch them fight over it.'

Then noticing my expression of disgust she exclaimed:

'What is the matter? Do you want me to leave a rat in there as a bedfellow for you?'

'A bedfellow?' I asked incredulously.

'Yes, a bedfellow! That is to be your room. You must live in there. It is too dangerous to have you wandering round the house; I have many callers. Why, is it not good enough for you?'

'Yes, yes, of course, madame. My French is not very good; I was not sure I had understood you correctly.'

She muttered something I took to be uncomplimentary, and went out and fed the rat to her hens, who screeched in appreciation, then fought to such effect among themselves that she returned to the house in great good humour.

'That rat was pregnant,' she said. 'In a few days there would have been another six or seven in the world. What a good afternoon's work!'

I forced myself to smile, and felt the time had come for me to try to establish better relations between us, loathsome creature though I felt her to be.

'I am grateful to you, madame, for your kindness in hiding me. You are very brave. If only I could speak French better I would not be such a nuisance to you.'

I spoke in a deliberate stammering fashion, hoping to encourage a belief that my knowledge of the language was so limited that conversation with me was not worth while. I was wasting my breath, however, for Madame was talkative by nature. No music was so sweet to her ears as the sound of her own voice. My attempt at bettering our relationship was successful, however, and by the time her husband returned home from a visit to a nearby town we were getting along famously. He was a small, lugubrious-looking man who, after getting over the shock of seeing me there – he had left early that morning, before Madame had been asked to hide me – treated me with exaggerated courtesy, which was in striking contrast to the attitude of his wife. He had no comment to make on my presence, for the simple reason that any comment would have been quite superfluous: his wife owned the house, the farm, and all the chattels, including himself. While I was with them he seldom answered her back though, to be fair to her, she treated him kindly, and once when he was unwell showed genuine concern until he was fit again.

My first week passed very slowly. I waited hopefully each day for the arrival of the young man, who had promised to return, but to no avail. The food was appalling, always some form of stew with a slice of black bread. Much of my time was spent .in the filthy hovel where Madame had killed the rat, and how I avoided some foul disease is a mystery to me. There was no proper sanitary arrangements in the house; so Madame gave me a bucket, and told me it would have to suffice for all my needs. The room was overrun with rats and nearly every morning there would be a drowned one in my bucket. The first two nights I did not sleep at all for fear that they might attack my face. Madame was very casual about emptying the bucket and I would usually have to ask her to do it. If it were not full, she would often leave it for two days, so that the stench was appalling. I could not empty it myself, since I was not allowed to leave the house. Every third day I would be allowed to wash in the kitchen; the water, having to be carried from a well, was considered too precious to be wasted on personal ablutions more than twice a week. Shaving was out of the question, apparently, for when I mentioned the possibility to Madame she told me to wait until I was due to leave.

'What is the point of shaving if you are not going out?' she said. 'And we know you are not going out!' Her husband shaved only occasionally and for special reasons, so my wish to do so struck her as ludicrous.

On the evening of my eighth day the young man called. Madame went out of her way to make him comfortable, and produced wine, biscuits and her best manners. He disappointed me by saying it would be at least a week to ten days before I could leave Amifontaine, but cheered me up by saying he wanted some particulars from me to enable him to get me an identity card.

'What is your Christian name?' he asked.

'Lionel,' I replied, 'though in the RAF I have always used my second name of Ronald, or Ronnie.'

'René,' he said. 'Yes, René. Your Christian name will be René. But your surname is Scott. What an impossible name! We can't do much with that!'

'Le Coq,' cried Madame, 'René Le Coq.'

For a moment everyone considered the possibility, and to my dismay it met with their approval, so from that day on I was René Le Coq. I could no doubt have persuaded him to give me another name, but did not want to reveal the fact that my French was so much better than Madame suspected.

It is odd to reflect that this was the first time anyone had asked me my Christian name; until now 'Monsieur' had sufficed for all occasions. It is true that Madame Leroux and my friends in Lor knew my full name but they never used it. Both Harry and I were always 'Monsieur' to everyone.

In the days that followed, life was more bearable. Madame allowed me greater freedom; she let me wander round the house during the day and I slept in the living-room at night. I began to understand how foolish it is to be prejudiced, merely because someone's manners and mode of life are very different from one's own. What gave me a true insight to this woman's character was an incident which occurred a few days after I had been christened René, and before my young friend (Pierre was his name) returned with an identity card for me. I was sitting playing with a pack of cards, and Madame was knitting. Suddenly her husband burst in through the back door crying: 'The Germans are here; René must leave at once.'

I was alarmed, and so was Madame. She went very white and, on rising to her feet, swayed unsteadily.

'Where are they,' she gasped, 'in the village?'

'Yes,' he replied. 'Questioning everyone and entering houses. René must go before they come in here.'

'Don't be stupid,' she said. 'Where can he go?'

'I don't care where he goes but he must not be found here. We will be shot!'

'He is quite right, madame,' I said. 'I must leave at once.'

'Be quiet, René,' she snapped. 'I said I would hide you. Do you think I will let you run outside straight into the hands of the Boche?'

'You have no choice,' shouted her husband. 'They will come in here and search for him; it will be the end of us.'

In his terror and panic he grabbed me by the arm and pulled me towards the back door. I did not resist, for it was obviously imperative that I leave at once. But Madame had other ideas, and grabbing me by the other arm pulled me away from him and into the storeroom.

'Quickly, lie down behind the grain. We will cover you up.'

'No, madame, I must leave,' I interjected.

'Be quiet! Do as I say,' and with a shove she sent me spinning into the corner.

'This is madness! Madness!' cried her husband, jumping up and down like a jack-in-the-box.

'Shut up!' she said. 'Go and see what the Boche are doing.'

He obeyed reluctantly, and no sooner had she thrown the first shovelful of grain over me than he was back.

'They are leaving,' he said sheepishly.

She stopped her labouring, dropped the shovel and ran to the front door, then started laughing.

'Oh, my poor little husband! What will you find to frighten yourself next? These are the soldiers who collect provisions for the Germans at St Erm. If they had come here it would have been to buy eggs.'

Monsieur was very embarrassed and sat down and put his head in his hands.

'I was thinking only of you and our little farm. I don't want to die in front of a firing squad.'

'Nor I,' she said, more sympathetically. 'Come, let us have a drink to celebrate our escape; we can do with it.'

Whilst all this talk had been going on I was busy ridding myself of grain. Madame had let me have the benefit of a good shovelful before her husband had appreciated his mistake, and it was in my hair, my ears and down the back of my neck. I emerged still picking and brushing it off, and added greatly to Madame's humour.

'My poor René, what have we done to you this afternoon? Come along! Let us all have a drink and we'll feel better.' The drink turned out to be green Chartreuse, and very good it was too. In my scant experience of these things, Chartreuse, like other liqueurs, was a drink taken at the end of a meal. I was surprised, therefore, to see Madame drinking it more or less by the glass. In no time at all she was very tight and most friendly.

'Come on, René, drink up!' she cried.

'No, thank you, madame,' I said. 'It goes to my head too quickly and then to my stomach. I have enjoyed it too much to want to spoil it all be being ill.'

'You are too practical, René. Like my husband, you

cannot enjoy the present because all the time you are thinking of the future and remembering the past.' She sighed philosophically, and after pouring herself another large one concentrated her attentions on her husband, who, having drunk as much as herself, looked even more mournful than usual.

'What is the matter, my little one? You look sad. That is no compliment to the good Chartreuse.'

He looked at her incredulously. 'What is the matter?' he exclaimed. 'You ask me what is the matter. I'll tell you. It is René. Why must you pretend hiding him is a joke?'

'Oh, go to bed!' she said. 'Have a sleep, and when you wake up the world will look better. After all, René will not be here for long.'

Grumbling, he took her advice and went into the bedroom, leaving us alone.

'Do not take any notice of him, René, he is very frightened.'

'He has good cause to be frightened, madame. What you are doing calls for great courage. I shall be grateful to you always.'

'You are a nice boy, René, and it is not right that you should be shut up here alone all day.' Then pausing momentarily, as something passed through her mind, she added: 'Would you like to see a pretty girl?'

'A pretty girl!' I said, surprised by the question.

'Yes, my little one, a pretty girl. It can be arranged.'

'I am not sure I understand, madame. Would it not be dangerous for anyone to know I am here?'

She laughed. 'No, it will not be dangerous. I'll invite a friend of mine and her daughter. Ah, what a pretty girl she is! You will have to be a very good boy, René, but you may look even if you cannot touch.'

She roared with laughter at her own witticism, and poured out the last of the liqueur. The bottle was almost empty, and only a few drops fell into her glass. She waited patiently as if expecting more to come.

'What is this?' she muttered, holding the bottle up to her eye like a telescope and peering into its green interior. 'It's all gone! What a pity!' and with that she downed the contents of her glass, and rising unsteadily to her feet said:

'I think I will have a little sleep. Call me if anyone comes to the door.'

She stumbled out of the room and into her bed. There was a gasp of surprise from Monsieur, a muttered 'Be careful,' and then silence.

They slept on long into the evening, so that instead of having our meal at about seven o'clock we ate at ten-thirty. I did not mind, for whilst they slept I listened to the BBC on the radio, a luxury usually denied to me on the grounds that it was too dangerous. On waking, Madame was, naturally, not as good-humoured as previously, whilst Monsieur did nothing to help things along. I could appreciate his feelings with regard to myself: as long as I stayed in the house his life was in jeopardy. He would probably have hidden a Frenchman evading the Gestapo and risked the consequences without complaint, but as he once said to me: 'If you are caught it may mean only a prisoner of war camp for you, but for Madame and myself it is the firing squad after they have finished torturing us.'

This fact had been in my mind ever since I'd landed in France, and I still think, as I did then, that we were not worth the courage shown and the sacrifices made on our behalf. Few of us were of any great importance so far as the war was concerned; there was no shortage of aircrew at this juncture. On returning to England, a man was interrogated and then sent on leave. He subsequently went on a lecture tour – if his escape had been interesting enough – or was posted to non-operational duties. Very few went on operations over Germany again.

The following morning, to my surprise, Madame was up bright and early in as sprightly a mood as ever. Her morning chores completed, she went out. When she returned it was to tell me that her friend with the pretty daughter was coming to tea. I was amazed, for I'd presumed all this talk about a pretty girl was some hallucination fostered by her over-indulgence of the previous afternoon.

Their arrival was the anticlimax of a day of preparation, Madame fussing around, Monsieur grumbling, and I doing my best to keep out of everyone's way. I was not the slightest bit interested in our prospective visitors, presuming that they would be rather wild country folk like my hostess. I hoped the whole affair would not be too embarrassing. When they arrived I got the shock of my life. The mother was a well-dressed woman of no more than forty, the daughter a slim graceful girl of perhaps seventeen. Madame introduced us, and when, after shaking hands with her mother, I held out my hand to this lovely creature I was aware of the reluctance with which she took it. When we sat down I could not help noticing how she took the chair farthest from me. Conversation was very formal, Madame doing most of the talking, and I sensed immediately that the relationship was not that of friends, but of servant and mistress. Madame had, I gathered, worked for this lady at some time. I said little, the chilliness of my reception being an experience new to me. This girl was too young and unworldly to hide the look of disgust always present in her eyes, and for the first time I fully appreciated how wild and unkempt was my appearance. The nicer she was, the more uncomfortable I felt. I found it difficult to accept humiliation with good grace, and felt very bitter towards Madame. When she began to boast, and it became obvious that self-glorification was the real object behind the invitation, I found it hard to contain myself. Nevertheless, the experience was probably good for me: a little humility is something we should all possess.

Later that night, Pierre came with my identity card and told me to be ready to leave in a few days. I was very elated, and spent every evening waiting for his knock. It was several days before he returned, but when he did it was to say I would be leaving the following morning for St Erm. Madame killed a chicken in honour of the occasion and Monsieur displayed an affability and humour of which I would not have believed him capable. The next day I shaved for the first time in a month and did not enjoy the experience, particularly since, once again, I had to use a rather blunt cut-throat razor. To cut my throat now would, I felt be singularly unfortunate, but uncommonly easy. When the time came to say goodbye, I asked Madame if I could make some financial contribution towards any expense she had incurred through hiding me, explaining that, like all airmen, I had a little French money. Both she and Pierre were most interested, and asked to see how much I had. On discovering a thousand francs, she took five hundred and Pierre two hundred and fifty; they insisted that I keep the remaining two fifty, explaining how dangerous it would be for me to travel without money. I was rather taken aback at losing three-quarters of my total wealth, for when I had made the same offer, both at Lor and La Mal Maison, it had been firmly rejected.

When we cycled off towards St Erm, leaving Amifontaine behind, I felt an exhilarating sense of freedom. The sun was shining, early blossom could be seen on the trees, the hedgerows were breaking into leaf, the air was fresh, and oh! so pure. This was spring, with all its expectancy of even better things to come. Much lay ahead, but I hoped the worst was over. As I watched the spinning wheel in front of me eating up the kilometres, it was hard to decide whether I was racing to St Erm or away from my last hiding-place. The first of March had seen me arrive in Amifontaine, the thirty-first saw me depart. When I'd arrived, the countryside had been in the grip of winter. As I left, it was bathed in the warm sunshine of early spring. A month of experience had come and gone, leaving me a little older, a little wiser, and a little farther along the road to freedom.

Five

St Erm was a railway junction, and our arrival coincided with that of several hundred German soldiers. They had disembarked from their train, and were, apparently, awaiting road transport to somewhere or other. We had to cycle through their midst, as they loitered in the sunshine, smoking and chatting, filling the square in front of the station and blocking the main road. Pierre rang his bell furiously, and I was surprised at the good-natured way they cleared a path for us. Many of them were men in their fifties, and some merely boys. They were, I learnt later, second-line troops, used merely for occupational duties. At this stage in the war, the Germans were using literally all their manpower – from sixteen to sixty. We turned up a side street, dismounted and pushed our bicycles through a back gate into a small garden, entered a house, and were greeted by Pierre's parents. His father appeared to walk with difficulty, and perhaps sensing my awareness of the fact, said, 'I suppose Pierre has told you I have only recently returned from a concentration camp?'

'I have told him nothing,' said Pierre, 'and you would be well advised to do the same. If he is caught, the less he knows the better. I don't mean to be rude, René,' he added, 'but it is no help to you to know all these things, and what you don't know you cannot tell anyone else.'

I was about to agree with him, but before I could speak his father broke in:

'Everyone in St Erm knows, it cannot do any harm for him to know also!'

'Of course it can,' said Pierre. 'If he is caught in a month's time and they torture him, he may tell them everything he knows, but what can he tell them about me?

My name is Pierre; I live in St Erm; I am young. Perhaps that would be enough for them to find me, but I don't think so. If on the other hand he can say that my father was in a concentration camp, it would give them the clue very quickly. Do you understand?'

His father indicated that he did, and was silent for some moments, but the desire to discuss his recent experiences was too much for him and he blurted out:

'They beat me every day, they gave me only bread and water, and then, when they found I knew nothing, kicked me out like a dog.'

Pierre was about to interrupt this passionate outburst, but before he could the wretched man burst into tears and left the room. His poor wife followed him, greatly distressed. It was one of the saddest things I had ever seen.

'I am sorry about that, René,' said Pierre. 'I am afraid my father will never be the same again; they have broken his spirit.'

He followed his parents into another room, and I could hear both he and his mother comforting the old man. I must say old, because this victim of man's barbarity to man was old, though barely fifty years of age. The torture chamber had accomplished in as many weeks what Nature would have taken twenty years to do.

They all returned presently, everyone behaving as if nothing unusual had occurred. An excellent meal followed, during which Pierre outlined his immediate plans, so far as I was concerned. I was going, so I learnt, to Buconville-Vauclerc, where I would spend a few days with a Resistance member, prior to moving on to Laon, a town and railway junction of some importance.

'I will put you on a lorry here in the main square. You will travel with a gendarme who will be responsible for looking after you, in so far as that is possible. If he should give you advice take it, without question, but give no sign that you know him. Remember, his task is a dangerous one. Are you quite sure you understand everything I have said?'

I said I did, but wanted to ask one or two questions about the gendarme and the lorry. Before I could, however, Pierre's father broke down once more, crying: 'If you are caught, do not tell them anything.' He grabbed me by the sleeve and shook my arm to emphasize the importance of what he said. Then, seeing the expression on his son's face, he let go of my arm and went on with pathetic dignity: 'I am sorry, monsieur; please forgive me. I have not been quite myself lately. You see I need a little time, a little more time.'

I made some comment I hope was appropriate, and with the aid of his wife changed the subject to something else. This was unfortunate, so far as I was concerned, for I longed to ask Pierre one or two questions in connection with his plan, and to discuss possible eventualities that might arise. But, out of respect for his father's feelings, I refrained, so that when we left the house I was not sure how I was to justify my presence in the lorry if asked to do so.

When we reached the main square, which was still full of Germans, Pierre led me to a shelter at what was obviously a bus stop.

'This is the place you are to return to if anything goes wrong. We will know to look for you here.'

'But suppose I cannot find this town; there are no signposts on the road.' I spoke, perhaps, too anxiously, for he looked at me scornfully.

'We can only do so much,' he said, 'some of it must be up to you.'

This attitude of his did not encourage me to ask any more questions, and presently I found myself apparently abandoned beside a dilapidated lorry in which sat a scruffy collection of labourers, several of them clearly conscripted workers from the Balkans. Pierre had stopped suddenly and said: 'This is the lorry, I must leave you here. Goodbye and good luck.' And with that disappeared up a side road, leaving me to my own devices. For a moment, an awful sinking feeling came over me. On what pretence could I mount the lorry, and where was the gendarme? I was, however, rather underestimating the Resistance movement, for suddenly a voice spoke behind me.

'Are you travelling in this lorry, monsieur?'

I turned round, and saw a gendarme in a green uniform. For a moment I hesitated, very unsure of myself.

'Monsieur Le Coq?' he inquired.

'Yes,' I said nervously.

He lit a cigarette, and turning away from me looked across the square as if something of interest had just caught his eye. He took a long drag, and then exhaled three or four magnificent smoke rings.

'Do not look so nervous, monsieur,' he said quietly and kindly from behind his hand as he raised the cigarette to his mouth once again. I did my best to relax and look natural, whilst he turned towards the lorry and spoke to a man who was approaching.

'Are you ready to go?' he asked.

The man nodded.

'Follow me,' said the gendarme, and climbed into the lorry. Without showing any interest or making any comments, the other occupants made room for us on the benches and we drove out of the town.

For some time we bumped along without conversation. The springs of the lorry had clearly been designed solely to support its pay-load, and with no thought or regard for the comfort of any human being it might be carrying. Hard wooden benches did nothing to help matters, and we were pitched and tossed all over the place. Conversation was practically impossible, not only because of the jostling we were receiving, but a broken silencer directly below us was making so much noise that to compete with its explosions was futile. All this was, of course, admirable from my point of view, and I noticed with relief that no one took any notice of me. Indeed, the only matter of general interest was the silencer, for not only was there the noise, but every time the driver changed gear black exhaust smoke belched up through the floorboards discharging oily fumes over us. Since, like lightning, it never struck twice in the same place, it was diverting to consider who the next victim would be.

After about ten minutes we stopped for petrol, and one of the men passed round a cartoon depicting a German officer sitting in a deck-chair staring out across the English Channel. The caption was something to the effect that he always went to the seaside for his holidays before the war, but could only stay for two weeks. Now he was in the

Army, life was one long holiday. I thought it was one of the most pathetic attempts at humour I'd ever seen, but everyone, including the gendarme, laughed heartily. I laughed as well, of course, because it was politic to do so.

Eventually we arrived at Buconville-Vauclerc, where my escort handed me over to yet another gendarme with whom I was to stay. An older man than my escort, and of more senior rank, he was clearly an ex-soldier. His fine bearing and rows of campaign ribbons told their tale, as indeed did his skin, tanned as it was by the African sun. His good-humoured eyes made their contribution to his opening conversational platitudes, making me feel I was truly welcome. Nor was my impression false, for no sooner had we drunk our wine and my escort had departed than he pulled up two chairs in front of a large open window overlooking his courtyard, and bade me sit down and give him an account of my adventures since arriving in France. He listened with interest, and then started to tell me the story of his life. I say started, for it went on for several days. He was a bachelor, an ex NCO of the French Army, and now a forest gendarme – a sort of game warden. He lived comfortably and I benefited accordingly. A young girl came every day and kept house for him. She was a plain girl, but kindly and sensible and an excellent cook.

'Please do not go to bed with her,' he pleaded. 'Good housekeepers are hard to come by, and if, when you go, you leave a pregnant girl the village would blame me. I could not tell them about you so I might have to marry her for the sake of my reputation.'

I assured him that no thought was farther from my mind and that the girl was quite safe.

'She is very plain,' he said, 'but you are here all day with nothing to do, and after a time she may appear more attractive. They are cunning, you know,' he added, 'very cunning. Why, she might make you sleep with her so as to make me marry her, heaven forbid!' The thought was unbearable; he was the most confirmed of bachelors.

Every evening a friend would call and play draughts with him. The man had only just been released from a concentration camp in Germany and walked with a difficulty it was painful to watch. I looked forward to his visits, however, for, their game over, we would sip our wine and listen to the BBC news in French, followed by the strange 'Les messages personnels', broadcast for the benefit of the Maquis. We would discuss the war and invasion, and go to bed feeling that the day of liberation was nearer.

One day, a young Frenchman turned up on a motor bike and introduced himself as Bob, a French secret service agent. At first, I was inclined to consider him a Maquis member with an inflated idea of his own importance, but when he produced two suitcases, one containing a neatly installed receiver and the other a transmitter, I quickly altered my opinion. These sets were of British manufacture, and had been dropped by parachute. Since, however, all the operating instructions were in English, and in technical language at that, no one in his area had been able to translate them. He had heard that there was a radio operator in hiding at Buconville-Vauclerc, and so had come to enlist my help. I was only too delighted to have something to occupy my mind, and soon had the receiver working. He was terribly pleased, and when I showed him how to 'back tune' the transmitter to the receiver he considered me a magician. He produced call signs, frequency charts and a host of relevant material, and asked me to transmit a coded message to England. I explained that this would not be possible with so small a set unless I had a decent aerial. I also pointed out that it would be an advantage to be on really high ground. He made notes of all I said, and told me he would find a suitable place from which we could operate.

He returned the next day, and after asking me very pointedly if I were still prepared to help him, gave me an automatic with fifty rounds of ammunition, and an encouraging slap on the back which nearly knocked me down. He had at least three revolvers of various bores, and goodness knows how much ammunition on his own person. What with our suitcases and coils of aerial wire we must have looked the most suspicious combination in France. We drove out of the village along the edge of the forest of Vauclerc until, we reached an area known as the Plateau de Californie, where we left the road and bumped up a cart track until forced to dismount. We continued on foot to the place he had chosen, which apart from being rather too open for my liking was well sited for a transmitting station. We erected our transmitter aerial quickly, using a very neat steel extension pole, and at an exact time began transmitting. This timing of transmission was most important, and 'rendezvous times' were arranged very carefully. Where Bob got his information from on this occasion I don't know, but from now onwards it came to us in code in the course of a transmission. When my call sign was acknowledged I was amazed, for I had never really expected an answer. To be passing and receiving messages in this surreptitious manner was almost too much like an extraordinary game, too much like the cinema's conception of underground activities and spying. Just as one never expected to be shot down, it was now, as then, difficult to believe that this was really happening to oneself. Bob decoded and coded messages, and for perhaps fifteen minutes I passed and received information.

In the days that followed we often went out into the forest, always to a different spot, sometimes chosen by the gendarme, who, of course, knew the area intimately. Only once did anything untoward occur.

We had left Buconville-Vauclerc and were travelling at high speed on the main road, prior to turning off into the forest. When going fast it was my custom to crouch behind Bob, so as to keep out of the slip-stream. Suddenly I felt him stiffen, and we braked violently. I straightened, and looking over his shoulder saw that the road was blocked by a company of German soldiers. 'We've had it,' I thought, for all these troops were armed, and a German officer stood in the middle of the road holding up his hand ordering us to stop. Bob had often told me that if trapped we must fight our way out, for he knew too much ever to be taken prisoner. I fingered my automatic and physically braced myself for the hail of bullets that I knew must soon follow. If we had been travelling slowly I think they would have followed, for Bob would probably have started the shooting. As it was, we were going so fast he was hard put to stop the bike a few yards short of the officer. You can charge a line of men in a car, but not on a motor bike, for if they don't get out of the way you will certainly come off in moving them. We slithered to a halt, and the officer came forward, smiling, as if pleased with his capture. Bob put his hands in his raincoat pockets and I knew why. I gripped my own automatic and prepared myself for the worst. There was a radio receiver strapped to my back; a coil of aerial wire round my neck under my coat. With a canvas bag containing still more aerial wire, a radio transmitter sat in a suitcase on the luggage carrier. We could not run for it, neither could we shoot twenty or thirty Germans. Surrender was impossible for Bob, and therefore for me. Time was running out fast, and as I prepared for the end I prayed. The officer spoke:

'I am so sorry to stop you like this, but my men are laying an electric cable across the road and it would be dangerous for you to go over it at speed.'

Bob took his hands out of his pockets. 'I am very glad you did,' he said, 'with the load we are carrying it wouldn't take much of a bump to have us off.'

'You look pretty well laden,' said the officer. 'What have you got in your cases?' He spoke pleasantly and without curiosity.

'Telephone equipment,' said Bob. 'The line has broken down near Neuville. That is why we were hurrying.'

'Well, don't let me delay you further,' and with an order to his men to stand back he waved us on our way.

Both of us were rather shaken by the experience and some miles further down the road stopped and debated whether we should call off the transmission. After some discussion we decided to carry on and took one of the small dirt roads that led into the forest. Bob knew exactly where we were going, the location having been suggested by the gendarme. After perhaps a mile we stopped and left the motor cycle in a woodsman's hut that Bob said was used only by our friend.

We continued on foot, climbing all the time, until we reached a clearing some two miles from the main road. There was evidence that this was a much used place for there were neat piles of logs stacked quite high and tractor marks joined the sawdust everywhere on the ground. It was an area used by the foreign workers who were employed in the forest and a long wooden table with crude benches acted as a centre point of the clearing. I suggested to Bob that although an excellent site it was rather exposed. 'There is no need to worry,' he said, 'our friend says no one will come here today.'

After checking that we did have the place to ourselves we unpacked our equipment and set up the transmitter.

I sent out our call sign and made contact almost immediately. I received a short message in code and was told that was all for today. Before Bob could decode the message we heard the sound of people approaching. Gathering the equipment together as quickly as possible, we moved behind one of the piles of logs. Two men appeared in the uniform of the Vichy police. 'They are collaborators,' Bob whispered. 'We can shoot if we have to.'

The significance of this remark was lost on me at the time but what Bob meant was that it was dangerous to shoot German soldiers because if one did reprisals were taken against innocent civilians, including women and children.

The two men began to wander round the site looking behind the stacks of logs – there were perhaps twenty – and it became obvious that we would have to try and escape before they found us.

'Listen,' said Bob; 'We must not lose this transmitter. I will try to get to the undergrowth over there,' he pointed to a particularly dense patch of forest behind us. 'Give me two minutes then make your way back to the motor cycle as quickly as possible; if we become separated you know the way back to Bouconville.'

He took the suitcase and ran towards the arboreal maze behind us giving me no time to ask even one of the questions racing, through my mind. I had no idea of the way to the gendarme's house for Bob always varied his route; I was not even sure that I could find his motor cycle for following someone through a forest is a very different matter to retracing your steps alone. The two policemen were not looking in our direction and Bob was making good progress but unfortunately he could not resist the temptation to look round and in so doing tripped and fell dropping the suitcase with a thud. 'Stop where you are', one of the two Frenchman demanded and they both drew their revolvers. Bob picked up the suitcase and to my surprise gave every indication of obeying their instructions.

I say surprise because at a range of some thirty-five yards he knew perfectly well that they had little chance of hitting him if he kept running.

The two men stood side by side making no movement and Bob, for his part, held his ground as he had been told to do. 'Come here', one of them spoke in a most contemptuous way, summoning him with a wave of his revolver.

Bob made as if to comply but then, suddenly, turned and ran for the wood zigzagging as he went. Both men opened fire. My reaction was immediate. In retrospect I do not know why, probably the sight of my friend in mortal danger made me behave instinctively, but anyway I fired several rounds at them. Their response was to dive for cover and hide behind the nearest pile of logs.

A silence ensued. No one fired at me. Bob had disappeared and our protagonists had gone to ground. What next, I thought, reloading my revolver. Perhaps a minute passed. Cautiously I peered round the corner of my shelter and looked towards our assailants. Suddenly a boot appeared from behind the pile of logs, its toe pointing skywards; it held this vertical position for a moment and then fell drunkenly to the side. There was a cry or a gasp followed by the sound of someone running into the undergrowth. 'He has run away, quick René we must go.' It was Bob's voice from the other side of the clearing. I picked up the receiver and joined him. He took my hand and shook it very firmly, his eyes betraying the emotion he was clearly controlling. 'We must go, they will be looking for us very soon.' We hurried back to his motor cycle in silence. When we reached the outskirts of Bouconville Bob stopped and turning to me said, 'René, we were careless, say nothing of this to anyone.' I took mild exception to the use of 'we', for after all my role was that of an unquestioning assistant, dependent on my master's judgement.

I kept my word and said nothing of the incident to the gendarme, however, a couple of days later he came suddenly into the kitchen and demanded, 'stick 'em up'. It was the only time he had ever said anything in English. It may have been both a joke and a coincidence.

Bob never referred to the incident again, indeed that single handshake was the only gesture he ever made in acknowledgement of what had occurred. I was content not to ask any questions, a choice probably denied to the owner of that foot.

Much later on I learnt that the police were actively engaged in a running battle with poachers. There was wildlife in the forests and food rationing saw to it that there were plenty of opportunists willing to take risks in order to supplement their families' rations. Our incident was probably reported as a brush with poachers and was therefore of no interest to the security forces, irrespective of the fate of that policeman.

The gendarme must have learnt of what had occurred and it is hard to believe that he did not equate the shooting with our presence in the area that day; nevertheless his 'stick 'em up' intervention was the only hint he ever gave of knowing anything. I replayed the incident in my mind time and again. My favourite fantasy was that the policeman was wounded and that his companion had not run away but had gone for help. It was an unlikely scenario, but for me, preferable to a more realistic one.

The next time Bob came he had an American fighter pilot with him. This American was a college professor. He spoke no French at all, and had, apparently, spent most of his time doing complicated equations. These involved workings had been found by the man who was hiding him, and had been passed on to Bob for examination. Such calculations were, of course, completely beyond everyone who saw them, so the American was regarded with suspicion. To settle the matter, Bob decided to bring him along to see me, so that I could ask the fellow what he was up to, and at the same time pass an opinion as to whether he was genuine or not. Before now, the Germans had been known to fire a few rounds of ammunition above cloud, prior to dropping an agent in British or American uniform. This man would seek help from the local people, and then, at an opportune moment, betray them.

It only took a few minutes' conversation for me to satisfy myself that this man was genuine. It was most interesting to compare notes with another evadee and to hear another point of view. This American was amazed that speaking French as I did I had not made for the Spanish frontier on my own. My point was that my chance of success was greater if I stayed with the Resistance, and anyway, I was doing useful work.

'They'll never let you go now,' he said. 'If they can't rustle up a radio operator without using a British airman they must be in a pretty bad way. What say we get the hell out of here tonight? You've got the lingo and a gun; what more can you want?'

I was attracted by the idea, but refused to go without telling Bob and my host, the gendarme.

'I can't just walk out on them after all they've done,' I protested. 'We must hear their side of the question.'

'To hell with their side,' he said. 'If they want to play secret service, let them.' Then seeing his remarks had not gone down well he added: 'Sure I know they've done a lot for us, but aren't we trying to liberate them? If they hadn't been so god-damned yellow in 'forty they wouldn't be in this mess now.'

I wouldn't accept his line of reasoning and insisted on telling Bob what we were thinking of doing.

Bob was up in arms at once.

'You can't go off like that, René; you wouldn't get a hundred kilometres without help, and besides you owe it to us not to be caught. I know you would not betray us willingly, but they would make you talk sooner or later; they always do.'

It was the last consideration that helped me make up my mind to stay, for I believe now, as I did then, that once the Resistance had taken you under their wing, it was one's duty to obey their instructions in so far as that was possible, and to avoid being caught; not for one's own sake, but for theirs. They were risking their all for us. Was patience too much for them to ask in return? The American could not see this line of reasoning.

'We don't get caught, period,' he said. 'We just don't get caught. Hell, how did a guy like you ever volunteer for flying duties?'

'That's by the way,' I said. 'How come you were ever shot down with this "I can't fail" philosophy?'

He looked angry. 'I was unlucky.'

'Yes,' I retorted, 'and if you are unlucky again these people will be more than unlucky – they'll be dead!'

'I'm no squealer, I'll not talk. Besides, they daren't torture an American or a British officer.'

'They dare do anything. In those civilian clothes you're not an American officer so far as they are concerned. You're a spy who says he's an American officer, and I'll bet more than one wretched spy has said something like that before now.'

'O.K.,' he said. 'I'll give 'em a couple of weeks, but if nothing has happened by then I'll go it alone.'

He was true to his word, for although Bob was able to keep him quiet for a month or so, by the simple expedient of moving him from village to village, he eventually tumbled to what was going on, and insisted on heading for the Pyrenees on his own.

What came of him I don't know, but whether he succeeded in reaching neutral territory or not, his action in trying to do so was, in my opinion, selfish in the extreme. He spoke no French, so would be unable to buy food or travel in public transport. It was unlikely that he could walk some eight hundred miles without help from French men and women, who might be acting out of compassion or patriotic motives and not be organized or equipped for hiding an evadee. He was, whilst living near Buconville-Vauclerc, in the hands of people who knew what they were doing, people who were part of an efficient and highly organized movement. He knew, for example, that American Intelligence had been informed of his whereabouts and that it was only a matter of time before he would be smuggled out of the country. Yet he could not wait, his fighter pilot temperament made him want to be up and doing. Frankly, he was lucky to be allowed to leave; some Resistance leaders might have considered such an action incompatible with their security, and a really difficult subject would have been told that he would remain where he was, or else!

The next Americans I met were very different from the first. They were young air gunners who had baled out of a Flying Fortress which had crashed in the forest of Vauclerc. I will call them Ed and Billy. One of them, Ed, had a badly burnt left arm and wrist, which, without proper medical treatment, had gone septic; yet he never complained, even though he knew that his arm might become gangrenous. The gendarme and his housekeeper both dressed the wound every day but it became obvious that we would need a doctor if the arm were to be saved.

For some reason no doctor was forthcoming and the gendarme was unable to contact Bob, who had actually left these Americans with us. 'If the worst comes to the worst, I will cut off his arm,' said the gendarme. 'It is the only way.'

Both I and Billy, were very concerned, not only for our sick comrade but at the prospect of assisting at an amputation. Ed's condition continued to deteriorate but fortunately a crisis was averted by the timely arrival of Bob.

Apparently there was no local doctor in the Resistance and the gendarme, although an active member, knew only his immediate associates. He could not, therefore, do very much on his own and was too proud to admit the limits of his knowledge and authority. The thought that a man might have lost an arm thereby, made me hope that I should never become really ill and unable to fend for myself. Bob arranged for these Americans to pass on down the line and Ed got the necessary medical treatment and kept his arm.

Many months later, quite by chance, I met both of them near Piccadilly Circus and we had a drink together. They told me how well they had been looked after in France and how grateful they were for the kindness their host had shown them. It was a pity, Ed said, that he would not be able to reciprocate this kindness but his friendship with a daughter of the house led her father to believe that a marriage would take place after the liberation. This was not Ed's intention, so he felt it would be imprudent to reveal his present whereabouts. 'The American army looks after its own', he told me, 'he'll never find me'. Billy had not been involved in this amour and told me he intended to show his appreciation in some tangible form but was up against the difficulty of doing so without revealing his friend's whereabouts. 'He suffered a lot and this kid was always fussing around looking after him. When he got to be well they kinda fell for one another; you know how it is! The poor guy suffered a lot, he had a bad time. He didn't know how serious she was, he meant no harm.' I wondered what view the girl would take of that explanation.

After the departure of Billy and his companion there was a brief period of tranquillity. The gendarme would go off in the morning, returning for lunch with an enormous appetite and much local gossip. This news was of passionate interest to his housekeeper, who, in return for doing his cooking, heard all the scandal and local politics. She would stand by his side agitatedly waiting for the climax of his tale, whilst he would drive her to distraction by taking a large mouthful of food or a long swig at his wineglass just before *le moment critique*. Only occasionally was any of this news interesting to me, so generally I got on with my meal in silence.

The food was always good, for as a game warden he was well placed to ensure that his table was endowed with the essential necessities of a gastronome's life. It is no exaggeration to call him this. Like very many Frenchmen, food and drink were practically the be-all and end-all of his existence. It was here that I was introduced to wild boar, a meat his housekeeper would prepare in numerous ways, all of them delicious. The wild boar is a large animal, larger than the domesticated pig, so when he shot one and smuggled it home in the dark, there was sufficient food for several people for a long time. To go into his cellar was rather like entering a butcher's deep freeze: great sides of bacon, fine hams, all preserved and cured in the correct manner, and all, of course, stemming from the same stock – the wild boar of the forest of Vauclerc. Another delicacy of which he was particularly fond, and the forest provided, was a small wildfowl, difficult to catch but well worth catching. Then, like most French peasants, he bred rabbits for eating, and was far too good a shot to miss even the fastest hare. All this hunting, even by a game warden, was illegal, but the risks he took – so he told me – only increased his appetite.

It was, I think, because of his larder that he was called on to hide evading airmen. Few Frenchmen had enough food for their own families, let alone an extra hungry mouth, and evadees were hungry people, for their food, poor though it might be, was often the only thing they had to look forward to, the only solace in the world of darkness and silence in which they often lived.

It was not from such a world that the next two Americans came. They were air gunners who had been shot down a few days previously. Before their parachutes reached the ground a small group of French men and women had been waiting for them, and within minutes of landing they were safely hidden. Neither of them had been able to keep apace of the situation, so quickly had everything happened. When they arrived in Buconville-Vauclerc I found them confused, impressed, astonished and mentally exhausted.

Their names were Virgil Marco, and Gene Snodgrass. Snodgrass was a tall, rather thin man of thirty-seven, with a slouching walk, hunched shoulders and sad expression. His eyes moved quickly beneath eyebrows of peculiar shape which arched themselves like bushy question marks. To speak to him was to evoke an eruption of physical response as his face and body twitched and contorted, wriggling and writhing like a tortured trout on a line or a dancing bear on a hot floor. Here was a man who wanted to please, and was pleased to be wanted.

Marco was nineteen and looked astonishingly immature for a man who had been to war. He was a fairly tall, well-built fellow, with close-cropped hair. Even in a French peasant's overalls he looked thoroughly American.

'Boy, have we taken a beating,' said Snodgrass. 'We haven't had time to think! Why, the kid here,' he indicated Marco, 'can't sleep, he just can't sleep.'

'Yes,' said Marco, 'it's been rough, but now we've found you I guess everything will be O.K., huh?'

'Why?' I asked.

He looked puzzled. 'Why? Hell, man, we've been in this country seven days! It's time we were moving out; my ma will be going crazy worrying about me.'

Snodgrass shook his head sympathetically. 'She sure

will, son, she sure will.'

'I can't do anything about getting you home, I'm an evading airman like yourselves, only I've been in France two months.'

'Two months!' they both shouted together. 'Say feller, what gives? For Pete's sake, let's wise up.'

I did my best to explain the working and methods of the Resistance and in doing so depressed them beyond measure.

'So that's how it is,' said Snodgrass. 'We've just got to sit it out.'

I explained that things were not as bad as they might seem to be, that we had comfortable quarters, good food and dependable friends; but it was to no avail. To them it was the end of the world, so easy had escape been since they had pulled their ripcords. They had arrived with Bob in the early morning, and shortly after our conversation I had to go out with Bob and our host to inspect a site the latter had suggested as a suitable place for our next transmission. We left the Americans in the care of the housekeeper with instructions to stay indoors and await our return. When we came back we found the girl waiting anxiously by the courtyard gate, looking most worried.

'These Americans are mad,' she said. 'They are walking about all over the house opening doors as if looking for something. They are very upset.'

I ran into the house and was met by Snodgrass.

'Say, am I glad to see you. I gotta pass water and there ain't no place anywhere; the kid's real bad, he's got pains.'

I kept my face straight and hurriedly led them across the courtyard, past a startled Bob and game warden, into the latrine.

Marco emerged almost immediately and went back to the house with the two grinning Frenchmen, but Snodgrass remained inside apparently wrestling with someone, judging from the snorting and banging that was going on. Eventually his face came round the door. 'Say,' he said, 'there ain't no chain!'

'No, there's no chain,' I replied; 'it's just a well with a seat on it; they've no proper sanitation in this part of the world.'

He shook his head sadly. 'Now ain't that something. I'll

say they need liberating.'

After lunch it was my custom to take a nap, there being nothing else to do, and on this day I had been sleeping for some time when I was wakened by a worried Marco.

'The old guy's missing,' he said. Thinking he meant the game warden I replied: 'So what?'

'So what! Say, you said we were to stay in the house, and he ain't in the house.'

'You mean Snodgrass?'

'Who else?'

'When did you last see him?'

'When we took our nap. I woke up and the old guy's gone.'

'He's probably in the latrine.'

'That's what I thought an hour ago.'

'Have you looked?'

'No. You said not to leave the house.'

'O.K.! O.K.! I'll look.'

I got up, and before going out walked to the window and looked across the courtyard to the latrine, which was situated in the centre of what had been stables. In one stable the warden kept his motor bike, in another his traps and hunting tackle. The centre door, the latrine, opened slightly and an anxious face peered one way, then the other. The figure of Snodgrass emerged clutching his trousers, his shirt tails outside them. Bending down so as to keep under the level of the courtyard wall which shielded him from the road, he surreptitiously entered the stable next to the latrine. There was a tremendous crash as he fell over the motor bike, a pause, and then the sound of the machine being righted. There was no light in the stable, the windows being boarded up, so when the door opened suddenly and Snodgrass sprawled across the yard it was obvious that another unseen object had crossed his path. He leapt to his feet and clutching his falling trousers charged through the first door he saw, which, unfortunately, was not that of the latrine. There was a loud clang as he ran full tilt into a disused water-tank, and a painful and pathetic cry floated across the courtyard.

'He's plumb crazy,' said Marco, not appreciating, as I did, what lay behind the various doors. Our friend emerged again still clutching his trousers and limped back into the latrine.

'Careful he don't bite you,' said Marco, when I made to go to the rescue. I crossed the yard and knocked politely on the door.

'Snodgrass?' I said.

'Yeh,' said a hoarse voice.

'What's the matter, are you ill?'

'There's no paper in here; I gotta have paper.' The voice was hoarse, the tone desperate. 'I gotta get out of here, I gotta have air.'

I rushed back to the house to find an old newspaper.

'What gives?' gasped Marco.

'He wants a newspaper,' I said.

'All this for a newspaper?' He looked at me incredulously.

'Not to read, you clot.'

'Wait a minute!' he said. 'You don't mean ... You can't!' His solemn face changed its expression. 'No! Oh no! This'll slay me!' And he collapsed in helpless mirth.

Snodgrass sat looking out of the window, philosophically considering the tops of the trees in the forest as they waved against the blue sky. From his expression, one might have felt he was wondering how a green brush could produce so deep a blue; how these undisciplined trees could paint their sky so evenly. But it was not so; more profound thoughts were exercising him, and at last he spoke pontifically.

'These people,' he said, 'have no sense of refinement.'

Later that evening, he was convinced that dishonesty was another charge he could lay against them, and I had great difficulty in keeping the peace between the game warden and himself when he caught the latter cheating at cards. The evening meal over, our host produced a bottle of spirit, distilled – by himself of course – from potatoes. It was most potent stuff, and one small tumblerful was more than enough for Marco and myself. Snodgrass, however, considered the first one the overture to a drinking session and found a ready and able collaborator in his host. He was completely outclassed, however, and whereas most of his faculties had soon deserted him, the game warden was only warming up. Something had to be done to stop them, and when the warden's friend arrived, as usual, to hear the B.B.C. news, I took the opportunity of suggesting a game of cards. The suggestion was well received, and we were soon playing pontoon, using buttons as counters. There was, for obvious reasons, no money involved, and from a gambling man's point of view the game was probably without meaning or reason. To Snodgrass, viewing the proceedings through an alcoholic haze, the loss of nearly all his counters was a serious matter, so when the warden, rather obviously, produced a card from under the table his wrath knew no bounds. 'This God-damned son of a bitch is cheating,' he roared suddenly, and springing to his feet glared angrily at his host and preserver. The warden looked first at him and then at me, and in a most unconcerned way asked: 'What's the matter with him? He appears to be upset.'

'You've given him too much to drink and now he wants to fight the German Army alone.'

This was the best I could manage on the spur of the moment, but it satisfied the warden and his friend and they both laughed. Snodgrass, of course, presumed they were laughing at him, and both Marco and myself had to move quickly to ensure no blows were struck. We restrained him and quietened him down whilst the two Frenchmen marvelled at the aggressiveness of this drunken, angry American.

During the days that followed an amusing situation existed, the warden rather admired Snodgrass for his aggressiveness, and the latter despised his admirer for his dishonesty. Snodgrass soon came, however, to see the comic side of the picture and even encouraged the warden to play cards again. The games that followed were terribly funny, for the warden always won, cheating in the most blatant manner. But the best was yet to come. Tired at the monotonous regularity with which this 'card-sharper' was allowed to win, Snodgrass tried a little sleight of hand and, as if it proved the adage of set a thief to catch a thief, the warden saw him, denounced him, and refused to play with him again.

Snodgrass enjoyed the joke as much as Marco and

myself, and even apologized for his misdemeanour. The warden accepted his apology with the air and dignity of a father confessor, but never played cards with him again. Snodgrass sagely remarked: 'That guy just can't have a sense of humour.'

He was wrong, as it happened, for the game warden did in fact have a sense of humour, though to be sure it was a strange one. One day, after Bob and I had been out with the transmitter, Bob decided to leave all the equipment with me, a thing he did not usually do. I saw no objection to this, and the warden being out we hid the equipment in his barn. Bob departed, saying he would not be back for a day or two, and I settled down with the Americans to await the warden's return. We had the radio and the sight of the housekeeper preparing our evening meal to entertain us, and with some good news from the Russian front to cheer us up we were, considering our predicament, in pretty good humour.

When the warden returned, also in good spirits, a cheerful evening seemed assured. The meal over, the warden produced his potent brew and we sipped and chatted whilst waiting the arrival of his friend. So accustomed was the warden to his evening routine that he never attempted conversation or suggested any diversion until his friend was safely installed in his usual chair with his pipe and a drink at hand. The housekeeper finished the washing and tidying up and bade us all good night.

'You can leave the door open. My friend will be here soon,' said the warden.

'Do you think it is safe to do so? Suppose someone else were to enter and find all these airmen here.' The girl clearly did not like the idea.

'Who are you expecting, the Gestapo?' His tone was most sarcastic. Knowing how futile it was to dispute anything with him when he wanted to argue she contented herself with a good night to everyone and left.

A strange thing about the warden was that he was most argumentative when in a good humour. When quiet and depressed, as he could appear to be if not feeling well, he was sweet reasonableness itself. The physiological explanation was probably that when fit and well and at peace with the world he had tremendous confidence in himself and his ability to deal with any problem or circumstance that might arise. After all, he was an independent individual, and as a senior NCO in Africa (and probably a very good soldier) he had, no doubt been powerful and important within his own domain. He had not married, so he told me, because he had never felt the need for a woman all the time; now that he was older and no longer as important as he had been, I think he sometimes found it difficult not to need a woman all the time; it was no longer as easy to find one on a part-time basis as it had been when he was younger and overseas. Today a housekeeper was a necessary compromise. Her importance was, however, only really apparent when he needed her: when he was ill, for instance. Tonight he was well and quite prepared to make an issue of anything.

Shortly after the girl had left, the sound of the front door opening and footsteps on the stone floor of the hall made him shout: 'Lock the door after you.'

A moment later, three men, unknown to me, entered the room and stood hesitantly just inside the door. They were as surprised to see us as we were to see them, and even the warden was taken aback, but only for a moment.

'Come in, come in,' he cried, jumping to his feet as if delighted to have more company. 'Sit down, sit down. Are there enough chairs? No! Oh, it doesn't matter; my friends are just leaving.'

I nudged the two Americans, who could not, of course, understand a word he was saying and they rose to their feet as I did.

'They are conscripted workers from Albania who have been working in the forest; they do not speak French. They are lonely for their homes, so I invited them here for a drink.' He beamed good-naturedly at us and then at the three visitors, who advanced smiling and shook us warmly by the hand. The warden shepherded us to the door. 'I will be back in a minute,' he told his uninvited guests, who sat down in our now vacated chairs.

He led us to the courtyard and the door which led out into the street. 'Take them to the barn loft and stay there,' he whispered to me. I led the Americans across the yard as quietly as I could whilst he remained at the door laughing and joking with himself in some extraordinary tongue. When he judged us to have reached the barn he made what I took to be a cry of farewell and banged the yard door and walked laughing back to the house.

We sat quietly in the barn waiting for the three strange men to leave, occasionally speculating in a whisper as to who and what they might be.

Some two hours later they left. The warden came into the barn and called me down.

'Who were those men?' I asked.

'Oh, they are men of this district who are Communists; they want me to join their party.'

'Are they in the Resistance?'

'In a sense, but we do not keep them informed of our secret work. They will be useful later on.'

I smiled to myself at the emphasis he put on the word *we*, thus identifying himself with the hierarchy.

'I suppose it would be best if we spent the night in the barn?'

He nodded. 'I think so. I will let you have some blankets, but first I must go and see what has become of my friend; he didn't come tonight.'

'By the way,' I interposed, 'I did not mention it before, but Bob and I hid the radio equipment in the loft.'

'But why?'

'I don't know, but Bob said you would understand.'

'Oh, yes, of course; I was forgetting.'

Even in the dark I could see him nodding his head knowledgeably. Bob had said nothing of the sort, as it happened, but the suggestion that there was something afoot about which lesser lights such as myself knew nothing, but of which I presumed he had full knowledge, was very satisfying to his ego.

'Are you going to join the Communists?'

He chuckled. 'No, I am a Catholic, and Communists don't believe in God.'

'Is that the only reason?'

'No, of course not. I don't like politics or politicians. France is better off without them. We need another Napoleon who will tell the people what to do. Politicians talk all the time. They are always telling you what they are

This photograph was taken just after my marriage in January 1945

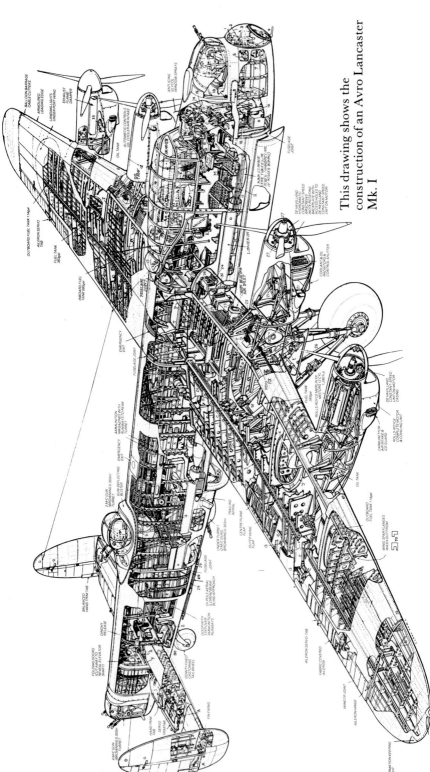

This drawing shows the
construction of an Avro Lancaster
Mk. I

When 'Able' was shot down, four cannon shells struck the under-fuselage from the rear-gunner's turret to just ahead of

BALLOON BARRAGE
CABLE CUTTERS

ARMOURED
LEADING EDGE

LANDING LIGHTS
UNDER PORT WING

EXHAUST
FLAME
DAMPER

AUTOMATIC CONTROLS
& COILS ON AIRFRAME

ANTI-ICING
GLYCOL
DE-ICING SPRAYS

OUTBOARD FUEL TANK 114gal

AILERON SERVO
TAB

OIL TANK

FUEL TANK
383gal

INBOARD FUEL TANK 580gal

RUDD-STARBOARD

DE HAVILLAND
HYDROMATIC
CONSTANT SPEED
AIRSCREWS

FUSELAGE
JOINT

FREE LINE
JOINT

EMERGENCY
EXIT

FUSELAGE JOINT

COOLANT & OIL
CONTROL SHUTTER

LUNKLEKON

RUM AIR INLET

AMMUNITION
MACHINES WITH
RUNWAYS TO REAR
TURRET

FUEL TANK
383gal

ROLLS ROYCE MERLIN XX
MOTORS 12 CYL

EMERGENCY
EXIT

2 M/C GUN
(BROWNING 0.303in)
REAR TURRET

GUN DEFLECTING
BLISTER

CARBURETTOR
AIR INTAKE &
ICE GUARD

DE HAVILLAND
CONSTANT SPEED
UNIT ON MOTOR
CASING

ROLLS-ROYCE
COMPLETE MOTOR
& COWLING JOINT

UNDER TURRET
(2 M/C GUNS
BROWNING 0.303in)

TRAILING
AERIAL

OIL TANK

CENTRE PLANE
FLAP

OUTER PLANE
FLAP

OUTBOARD
FUEL TANK 114gal

WING SPAR FLANGES
FUEL TANK

BALANCED
HAND TRIM TAB

DINGHY
RELEASE

FOLDING DOORS
(CUT AWAY TO
REVEAL ELEVATOR
SHAFT)

D/F POLE AERIAL
(LOW FREQUENCY)
BLIND APPROACH

FUSELAGE
JOINT

DOOR WITH
AMMUNITION
RUNWAYS

DINGHY FIXED
TAIL WHEEL

AILERON SERVO TAB

FABRIC COVERED
AILERON

HAND TRIM
TAB

SERVO
TRIM TAB

4 M/C GUN
(BROWNING 0.303in)
TAIL TURRET

FIN FIXING

HINGE TIP JOINT

AILERON HINGE

FORMATION KEEPING
LIGHT

NAV. LIGHT

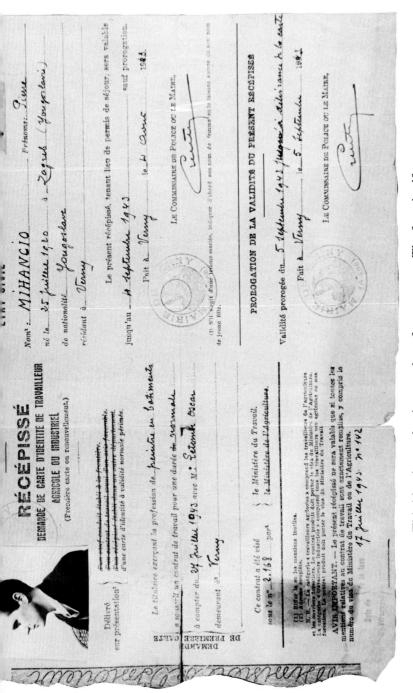

This identity card twice saved me from capture. The form itself was stolen and the rubber stamps on it skilfully forged

A Lancaster identical to 'Able' releasing its bombs over a target in northern France. It was our inability to open the bomb doors, as seen in this picture, which forced us to abandon the aircraft. Our incendiaries were ignited around a 4,000 lb. bomb

The Lancaster's ability to carry around eight tons of bombs to targets in Germany and still climb to over 20,000 ft., gave it an operational advantage over both the Stirling and the Halifax. We normally carried a live 4,000 lb. bomb, and the balance, approximately four tons, in incendiaries

This photograph was taken during the Berlin Airlift by a colleague who had just bought a Leica for 100 cigarettes

TARGET   M.A.N. (MASCHINENFABRIK AUGSBURG
NURNBERG A.G.) - AUGSBURG.

NOTES.   11/39.

View from North East.

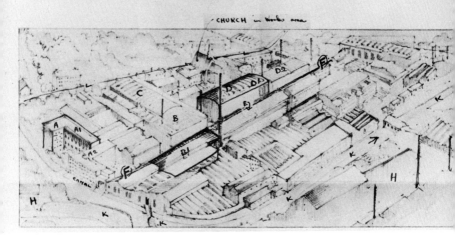

When Wing Commander Nettleton won his Victoria Cross for
leading 44 Squadron on a low level attack on Augsberg, these were
two of the charts handed to crews at the 'briefing'. We were to bomb
from 20,000 ft. so consequently our charts were of a more general
nature although the targets were largely the same

The Lysander Mark II was much used by the Intelligence services because of its ability to land and take-off in very short distances. The empty cockpit I was not 'important enough' to occupy can be seen in this illustration

Prior to take-off on a bombing mission, aircraft were controlled by an operator in a black-and-white caravan called the 'Domino'. Communication between the 'Domino' and the control tower was by telephone and in order to maintain radio silence, all instructions to the waiting aircraft were given by Aldis lamp

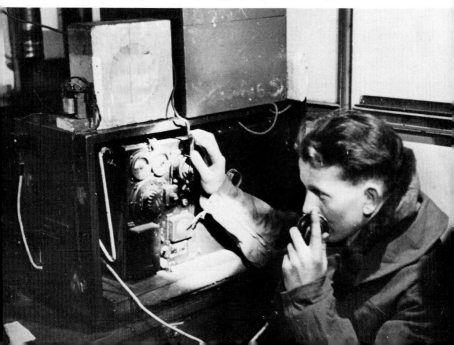

Dr and Jacqueline Boury on a visit to London during the summer of 1946. This was our first meeting after almost two years

going to do, but they never do it. We need a strong man and one policy; Frenchmen cannot compromise.'

'Tell me what language you were speaking.'

'Arabic.'

'Were you not afraid they might perhaps know some Arabic or wonder how it was you could speak that language?'

'They are simple peasants, they have no experience of the world.'

'Oh, I see. But will they not tell others that you were entertaining three Albanians?'

'That does not matter; the forest is full of foreign workers. You travelled with some of them the day you came here.'

I agreed that was so, and rejoined the Americans while he went off to see what had become of his friend.

'Well?' asked Snodgrass.

'There's nothing to worry about; they were only Communists who wanted to see if he would join their party.'

'Those guys were Russians?'

'No, French Communists.'

'French Communists?'

'Yes, Frenchmen who are Communists; there are quite a lot of them in France.'

'What did he say?'

'He said no.'

'Why?'

'Because he says Communists don't believe in God.'

'That's a good reason. But does he?'

'He's a Catholic.'

'Yeh! Well, I hope he confesses about his card games, the old hypocrite.'

'Card games or not, he's a pretty good Joe hiding us all like this. He's for the high jump if the Krauts ever catch him.'

This was one of Marco's rare utterances, and, as was often the case, very much to the point.

'Sure, I know all that; but he still cheats at cards and he ain't got a sense of humour.' Snodgrass meant this last statement to end the conversation for the present, and it did. We sat in silence, but not for long. Snodgrass spoke again: 'Man, I gotta pass water.'

'You and me,' said Marco.

'He's bringing us some blankets presently. I'll ask him if we can go down to the latrine then.'

'And if he says no?' Marco clearly expected an answer in the negative.

'Then,' said Snodgrass with a philosophical sigh, 'we'll just have to let it die in sleep.'

A little later the warden returned, locked the yard door and went into the house. I did not hear him come out again, so his quiet whistle from the barn ladder surprised me.

'Here are your blankets,' he said, handing up three blankets and three pillows. I took them, thanked him, and asked   how his friend was. He gave a little laugh.

'He is quite all right. On his way to see me this evening he heard a drunken man shouting in a strange tongue outside my door and being frightened went home.'

We both laughed quietly, though when the warden explained the joke to me, thinking, perhaps, that I had missed the point, I found it hard to subdue my mirth.

'What goes on?' I heard Snodgrass muttering, and remembering his predicament asked the warden if we could use the latrine.

'No, you had better stay here in case anyone is about.'

'What do you suggest, then?'

He considered for a moment. 'You know what a Frenchman would do in a barn?'

'Yes, but they are not Frenchmen.'

'Very true, wait a minute.'

It was fully five minutes before he returned and handed a bucket up to me.

'Here's a torch as well; use it with care and only if necessary.'

I thanked him and said good night.

'There's something funny here,' said Snodgrass. 'Lend me the torch.'

I handed it over and he shone it on the bucket. It was a truly remarkable sight. The entire rim of the bucket had been decorated with a blue satin ribbon. The decoration had been carried on to the handle where it culminated in a large lover's knot. For a moment Snodgrass held the torch steady as if ensuring that he really saw what he thought he saw, then he switched it off.

'Well,' he said, 'he still cheats at cards!'

The following day the warden moved the radio equipment to another hiding-place. Whilst I was handing it down to him the thought that the bucket was as yet unemptied crossed my mind. The Americans were already back in the house, and having been called down by the warden with instructions to cross the yard quickly, they had, not unnaturally, left the bucket behind. I handed down the last item, then asked: 'What about the bucket?'

'Ah, the bucket; yes, pass it down to me.'

I did, and to my surprise noticed that the ribbon had gone. He said nothing, but a little later that morning when his housekeeper complained to him that a satin ribbon of hers was missing, he suggested that perhaps one of the Americans might have it. On discovering that it was in Snodgrass's possession she was very cross. The poor man's attempts to explain how it came his way were doomed to failure before he began: without a word of the language to help him he was lost, for it was hardly a tale one could recount in sign language.

'What were you going to do with it, anyway?' I asked.

He shrugged his shoulders: 'I was hoping to think of something, but I ought to have known better; that old guy just can't lose.'

I liked those Americans: the fact that we had practically nothing in common enabled me to appreciate their virtues more easily than would have been so with two Englishmen. They found the France they had seen primitive and backward in terms of sanitation and general amenities, and therefore judged the whole nation accordingly. It was no good my trying to explain how rich a country this was in terms of literature, music, art and, in particular, civilized living; for they would not believe that such a country would allow the people to live as these people lived: without lavatory chains, water taps and electric light. When I argued that equally primitive conditions existed in America I was answered with: 'Maybe they do, but at least

we eat our meat and vegetables together.' It became clear
that it was not so much the primitive aspect that upset them,
as the fact that things were different. The first time we had a
meal together, Marco commented that I used a knife and
fork 'like the folks in England'. My being British had
nothing to do with it; it was not the American way; it was,
therefore, peculiar if not actually wrong. That anything
American might appear strange or garish was outside the
scope of their experience and was never considered. Yet, as
I have said, this narrowness of outlook showed up the best
side of their characters: they never asked for vegetables
with their meat, but ate the two courses separately. They
never, by word or gesture, made the game warden feel his
home and surroundings were other than what they were
used to. They never displayed or gave vent to their feelings
in any shape or form – save on one occasion when
Snodgrass was drunk – and they always treated the housekeeper with respect and courtesy. You may argue that such
conduct is only indicative of good manners, and has
nothing to do with character or courage; that is so, but their
outward cheerfulness when depressed, their bravery when
frightened, their patience when both were impatient for
action and no action was forthcoming, were endearing in an
intangible way. This side of their natures showed up particularly well the day I left Buconville-Vauclerc on my way to
Laon. The night before my departure, and before I knew I
was leaving, the game warden came home with the news
that we were all going to Laon the following day. Everyone
was elated, and the wine flowed after supper when our
good-natured host and his friend wished us *bon voyage*. We
were all up early the following morning, as Snodgrass put it,
'raring to go', so when Bob arrived (on a small motor bike)
with the news that, due to a change of plans, only I would be
leaving, they were more than disappointed. I was really
sorry on their account, and would have been even more
sorry, but for the news that I was going to drive myself to
Laon on the small motor bike. I could drive a car, but had
never ridden a motor bike solo, and though I don't pretend
it is a feat requiring any particular skill, most people would,
nevertheless, prefer an easier proving-ground than the
roads of an enemy-occupied country, particularly when

only those in possession of a special permit were allowed to
travel at all.

I paid great attention when Bob explained the working
of the gears, throttle, brakes and so on, and after a run
round the yard thought I could get away with it. If I had
not felt sure of myself, it would have only been right to
admit my doubts, but if I were caught on this occasion no
one else would be directly involved and so the chance was
worth taking. This, rightly or wrongly, was how I reasoned
and, after lunch, prepared to leave. Bob was taking the
game warden's bike and would precede me; I was not,
however, to give anyone the impression that I was
following him; and if he were to stop, I was to carry
straight on as if travelling alone. My motor bike belonged
to the Resistance and was not traceable. Bob told me to say
I had stolen it if I were captured. This was the obvious
story to tell, but I doubted if the Germans would be
convinced: after all it is difficult to find, let alone steal, an
ownerless, unregistered motor bike in good condition, and
filled with petrol, which was strictly rationed.

I said my farewell, and was very touched by the warmth
and sincerity of the good wishes of the warden and his
housekeeper. Snodgrass and Marco were also buoyantly
cheerful in the true American tradition of making the best
of things; yet my departure robbed them of an interpreter,
and as Snodgrass said: 'Me and the old guy don't trust one
another and we gotta talk in sign language.' I owed it to
Snodgrass to do something, so taking the warden aside I
explained that my friend was concerned that there was a
loss of confidence between them, and now that I was
leaving he felt without an interpreter mutual confidence
might not return. The warden appreciated the point and
as a gesture of good will fetched up some tobacco from the
cellar, produced cigarette paper, and invited Snodgrass to
roll a cigarette. This Snodgrass did, with trembling
fingers; the thought of a 'drag' gave his life meaning again.
It was a pity that the warden omitted to tell him that this
was not true tobacco, but a leaf, which in his opinion, after
being treated with vinegar and dried in the sun, was as
good. Unfortunately this was not an opinion with which
Snodgrass concurred, and his expression, as he inhaled,

was that of a man who has just discovered the eighth wonder of the world and wished he hadn't. He ex- haled like a tube blowing a valve.

'Give it to me straight, boy,' he said, 'is it a joke or does the old fool think this is tobacco?'

'It's not a joke, he means to be kind.' I spoke quickly and with emphasis. Snodgrass smiled, and nodding to the warden said: 'It's great, just great.' The latter did not understand and turned to me for a translation.

'He says he likes it and thanks you.'

The warden smiled. 'Good, tell him he can have enough for six cigarettes a day.'

I passed on the message.

'I can't figure this guy out,' said Snodgrass. 'Why don't he just shoot me, it'd be easier and quicker. Six a day! Why, I might live a couple of weeks!'

'He figures he don't need you for that long,' said Marco, 'but just as soon as that little old wild boar is finished I reckon it'll be you, with pickles.'

'Yeh,' Snodgrass shook his head sadly. 'If he can smoke this stuff I don't put nothing past him. I'll be down in the cellar with the hams, smoked hams.'

Seeing that Bob was impatient to leave, he held out his hand. 'Look after yourself, feller, and remember, we'll be in there pitching for you.'

'Yeh, that goes for me too,' said Marco, 'and if you make England see the Army lets my ma know I'm alive and kicking.'

'The same goes for my old man,' said Snodgrass.

I promised, and to subdued ironic cheers from the two of them motored out of the yard.

Once on the open road I became so nervous that it was several minutes before I realized that the bike was in bottom gear. I changed up, thus allowing a puzzled Bob, who had been riding very slowly wondering why I did not come on, to accelerate. We sped on at a good pace and by the time we reached Chermizy, the first village on our route, I was riding confidently.

It was disturbing to find, however, that the local populace were regarding me with more than passing interest. The truth of the matter was that they were curious. So few motor bikes were on the roads in those days that anyone on one was worthy of temporary observation.

To me, of course, such interest seemed indicative of dire consequences. I must look suspicious, and the first German soldier would undoubtedly stop me. I adopted what I hoped was an air of sublime indifference, and motored with a casual disregard for my surroundings. So casual, indeed, that an old woman who crossed the road without looking left or right was nearly run over. In avoiding her I stalled the bike and my attempts to restart it whilst she railed at me gave much innocent pleasure to the local population. When I did get going, Bob was no longer in sight, and a worrying five minutes passed before he appeared ahead. In catching him I over-revved the engine and it began to seize up; fortunately I knew what was happening, and stopping and dismounting quickly, kicked the flywheel furiously for some minutes to keep it 'free' until the engine cooled down.

Bob was now far away and all hope of making Laon appeared to have gone. There was no point in going there unless to meet someone and, of course, I had no idea where Bob was taking me. I would probably have returned to Buconville-Vauclerc, but the sound of an approaching vehicle sent me motoring up the road with heart pounding. It turned out to be a German staff car, and all the occupants, with the exception of the driver, turned and stared at me. There were two German officers and two girls in uniform plus the driver. They motored alongside for a few moments and I felt sure they were about to stop me, but they were, apparently, only enjoying a joke at my expense, for after a minute or two the car swerved and accelerated, almost putting me in the ditch. They were all laughing like mad; a typical act of Teutonic humour. Little did they know how relieved they left me, and how the laugh was really on them.

I decided to press on and hoped to find Bob; after all, he did not want to lose me! It was a good thing I did, for wondering what on earth I was doing he had turned back to find me, and going round a corner we passed each other travelling in opposite directions. Thereafter there were no more excitements and even when following Bob through Laon, which was full of German soldiers, we had no incidents. On arrival at our destination – the house of a Resistance member – I learnt that we were picking up an American and motoring on to Chauny as soon as lunch was over.

The American duly turned up; he was very young and confused. It took me several minutes to convince him that I was also an evadee airman. Once convinced he was very affable, but until then rather sullen and suspicious. He had only been in France a short time but had spent most of it in a dark cellar. The prospect of a ride across occupied territory on the back of a motor bike apparently gave him no concern.

'It's doing nothing that drives me crazy,' he said. 'I like action.'

Our route from Laon to Chauny was the more or less direct one: Molinchart, Cessières, St Gobin, Sinceny, Chauny. From Cessières to St Gobin it was heavily wooded, and in this area, Le Haut Forêt Coucy, an active Maquis group was operating. If we had to leave the road and take refuge in the forest our chances of escape were good, or so Bob said. The first part of our journey was uneventful, but just before Sinceny we ran into the back of a German convoy of briskly driven trucks. We were now in flat open country with no shelter in sight, and I quickly reasoned that my only chance of escape if challenged lay in turning round and driving in the opposite direction. It would take them some minutes to turn a truck round, for the road was narrow, and so far as I could see there were no escorting vehicles. My problem was not quite so simple, however, for it was quite possible that Bob would stop if challenged and show his identity papers. Both the American and myself had forged identity cards and Bob might feel therein lay our best chance of escape. Should Bob be stopped, and I turn round and run away, they would almost certainly detain him and the American on suspicion. On the other hand, would it be any use if I turned their double act into a trio? Neither did the fact that we were armed help, for their cargo being apparently valuable, there were armed men in each truck.

Suppose Bob, seeing the game was up, made a fight for it – he had always told me he could not be taken prisoner – what should I do? Should I turn round and escape – as I might be able to do – or should I ride in, gun blazing, to a certain death? It was obvious that my contribution would achieve nothing – there must have been a hundred men with the convoy. Yet, if I ran away, it would be to brand myself a coward, although a practical and sensible one. If, on the other hand, I died fighting for and with my friends, it would be a hero's death, brave and honourable, but perhaps foolhardy, for it would avail nothing. Today I do not know the answer to the problem that confronted me all those years ago, nor do I know what I might have done, let alone what I should have done. Questions concerning war, like war itself, are often futile.

Bob drove on past truck after truck whilst I hung back watching, waiting, then suddenly I accelerated past the last truck and was now in the convoy with my friends. Faces filled, I was sure, with interest stared at me from the back of the truck in front: frightened people always exaggerate their importance. I passed one truck, then another and another, always to find a fresh row of staring eyes, each seeming more interested in my progress than the last. Bob, I noticed, had now passed the convoy and was pressing on at a good speed, a speed my small bike could not match, indeed it took all my engine's revs to pass each truck, the screaming of my two-stroke challenging their shrieking back axles. At last I was in front, in effect leading the convoy.

Until now it had been fairly easy to choose a moment to pass one of these trucks: they were all motoring at a uniform speed, and if any driver objected to my overtaking him there was little or nothing he could do, with the rear end of the preceding vehicle just in front of his radiator. No such restriction was imposed on the leader, however, and he decided to have some sport at my expense. The maximum speed of my bike was about seventy kilometres per hour and he could certainly exceed this. He pulled out, and hooting aggressively began to pass. Without the power to resist his challenge there was little one could do on a fairly straight road, yet I wanted to keep out of this convoy at all costs. My throttle was wide open; the engine doing its best. Nevertheless it had practically seized that morning and was suspect if driven hard for any length of time. Not content with passing, the driver now began to crowd me as if meaning to put me in the ditch. This was the second time I'd had to tolerate such treatment in the last few hours, and, in my anger, all fear departed. 'All right,' I thought, 'put me in the ditch.' We motored along side by side, I refusing to give an inch, and he, although probably peeved at my stubbornness, clearly did not intend to carry out his bluff. Neither did he intend to make my lot any easier by passing, and when I throttled back he did likewise. Bob, puzzled by the hooting, had slowed slightly and the American was looking back and, no doubt, trying to explain what was happening. This must have bothered the driver of the truck, for suddenly he lifted his foot and slowed down and I shot ahead. Our theory afterwards was that he did not connect the two motor bikes, and seeing Bob slow and the American look back, felt there might be independent witnesses if I lodged a complaint. For all he knew, we could be collaborators, not only friendly but useful to the occupation authorities. His sudden slowing caused consternation in the trucks behind him, and at least one shunted the preceding vehicle. There was a shrieking of brakes, the sound of a collision, then angry shouting as the convoy stopped. I did not look back, much as I wanted to, but put my head down in true racing fashion and forced the speedometer needle past the seventy kilometre mark; I was going to put as much distance as possible between that convoy and myself, whatever happened. Shortly afterwards we reached the main Chauny-Soissons road, and turning on to it motored quietly into the town. We never saw or heard any more of that convoy.

It was irritating to find that no one thought much of my experience: these people had lived such dangerous lives for so long that any incident from which one emerged unscathed was worthy of only brief recognition. In fact, the only pleasure they derived from my story was the thought of one Boche running into another.

Six

Our stopping-place in Chauny was the garage of a M. Logeon. After exchanging the usual pleasantries with the owner, his wife and his pretty daughter, we were taken into the garden at the back and introduced to a Mlle Jacqueline Boury, at whose father's house we were to spend the night. To our surprise and delight she spoke excellent English, and quickly explained how we were to follow her through the town to her home. It transpired that her father was a local doctor, active in Resistance affairs. Bob said goodbye and told us we would hear from him in a few days' time, and that meanwhile we would be interrogated by a secret service agent who would pass us as free to go on to Paris or otherwise.

'If it is otherwise you will not see me again.' He laughed wickedly and winked.

I translated his remark to the American, who looked puzzled. 'Don't get it; what does he mean?'

'He means that if you are a German agent the Resistance has its own way of getting rid of you.'

Jacqueline spoke hurriedly. 'But now you must come home with me, before my father's evening surgery begins.'

We shook hands with everyone and then followed her at a discreet distance.

'Say,' said the American, 'what's all this German agent stuff?'

'Oh, it's nothing you need bother about.'

'Man, I am bothered. If some bum says I'm a German it's the high jump for me.'

'There's no risk of that; it was a joke.'

'Yeh! Well, they've got a funny sense of humour, see! They thought you and that convoy was funny. Well, I didn't see the joke and I was there!'

At this point I had to quieten him, for we passed some

people in the street, but he was still worried.

We were soon safely installed in the doctor's home and for the first time in ten weeks the joys of modern plumbing were mine for the asking. Madame Boury gave us coffee and biscuits and made polite conversation in halting English. To drink from a good china cup again, to sample and enjoy quality furniture and furnishings, to see a piano which I longed to play, the pleasing personality of sixteen-year-old Jacqueline; all these things made the prospect of a stay here attractive and inviting. The arrival of the doctor only strengthened this view, for here was a man, hale and hearty, who fairly oozed good will. His English was excellent, and over dinner he expounded his views on music, art, literature, travel and human experience. It was both a joy and an education to sit at his table. When our meal was over, he produced a fine cognac, and we sat in a small circle round the fire warming our brandy glasses in our hands. The swirling contents sent up an intoxicating bouquet which lulled us into a happy state where, temporarily, the trials and tribulations of war were forgotten, and good wine and good company seemed the happiest combination on earth.

The following afternoon we were interrogated as promised. Shortly after lunch two men came to the front door with Mlle Logeon, and after being introduced to Jacqueline and her mother – the doctor was out – asked to see us separately, the American first.

Due to a misunderstanding we went in together, the American nervously, I in boisterous good spirits, filled with *bonhomie*. The American introduced himself and shook hands. I waited until he had finished, and then thrusting out my own hand said confidently: 'How do you do, I'm Scott.'

'Well, Scott, would you mind waiting outside until you've been asked to come in.'

The speaker was a tall man, probably in his thirties, immaculately dressed in an arty sort of way: pale grey suit of perfect cut, white shirt with spotted bow tie, and a matching handkerchief generously exposed in his breast pocket. His handsome face wore an irritated frown, and when I did not immediately comply with his request he snapped: 'Do you mind?'

'No,' I said, completely taken aback. 'But I understood you wanted to see me.'

'When I've finished with this American. Now if you don't mind, please.'

He made a gesture towards the door, and feeling thoroughly deflated I left the room.

When my turn came it was with difficulty that I controlled my temper.

'Ah, Scott! Sit down. Now tell me, when were you shot down?'

'The 25th of February.'

'Nonsense, there were no operations that night.'

'There were, we bombed Augsburg.'

'You bombed Augsburg?'

'Not personally. I was shot down on the way there.'

'What was your aircraft?'

'A Lancaster.'

'Your squadron?'

'I'm not sure you need know that.'

'I know it was 44.'

'Then why ask me?'

'You went to a public school?'

'Yes, why?'

'I'm asking the questions.'

'Sorry!'

'Where do you live?'

'Richmond.'

'Which Richmond?'

'Surrey.'

'How would you travel by tube from Richmond to Piccadilly Circus?'

'By District Line to Hammersmith, then change on to the Piccadilly Line.'

'When were you last on leave?'

'Just before I was shot down.'

'Tell me the name of one film showing in the West End.'

'*For Whom the Bell Tolls.*'

'Thank you, Scott.'

He stood up and smiled.

'You rather lost your temper, didn't you?'

'Well, you were pretty rude.'

'I meant to be; an Englishman losing his temper is a quite distinctive thing. The Germans do it differently.'

'You didn't really think I was a German, did you?'

'No, but my job is to make sure.'

'Tell me, how did you know my squadron?'

He looked across at his companion, a small man in a dark suit, and they exchanged smiles.

The doctor arrived before they left, and over a glass of wine my interrogator chatted freely, but his partner contented himself with an occasional yes or no and nothing more.

After they'd gone I turned to the doctor: 'His French was pretty good, wasn't it?'

'But, of course, he is a Frenchman.'

'No, no, he is very English and his accent is unmistakable.'

'My dear friend,' the doctor smiled kindly, 'that man was a Frenchman; no foreigner could deceive me.'

To this day I don't know the answer.

The following day the American left. M. Logeon collected him and took him to a farm some miles from Chauny, where he stayed until liberated by his compatriots some months later. To my surprise I stayed with the Bourys. They had, apparently, taken a liking to me, and the doctor told M. Dromah, the local Resistance leader, that he would hide me for a while if it would help the movement. Dromah had been pleased to accept the offer: he was finding it hard to persuade people to hide evadees at this time.

Seven

My stay with the Bourys was a happy one. At first, I thought it was to be short, for Bob had told both the American and myself that we were *en route* for Paris. But plans were changed, just as they had been when I was staying in Amifontaine, and what started off as a few days became a month. Not that I had anything to complain about. True, the desire to get home was very strong, and all these delays were frustrating, but whereas most airmen in hiding had to struggle with fear, loneliness and boredom, my existence was comfortable and interesting. The doctor decided that I should get out and about, so that should anyone chance to see me, that fact in itself would not arouse suspicion. First, however, he felt that really good forged papers were necessary.

'After all, René, you have a foreign accent which even a French-speaking German might detect. Your French identity card is next to useless. What you need is a foreign worker's identity card, then people will accept your accent without question. Leave it to me, I will arrange everything.'

He did, too, and when my new card came I was Pierre Mehancio, a conscripted Yugoslav house-painter.

'To any German, house-painting must be a noble profession. After all, was it not the profession of their Fuehrer?' The doctor loved his joke; nevertheless, I often felt 'farm labourer' would have been a less definite occupation.

Sometimes, I would go shopping with Jacqueline, and soon word got back to the doctor, warning him that his daughter had been seen in company with a young foreign worker. How he enjoyed hearing this. Several times I went to the cinema with Jacqueline and her mother – we would go in separately but sit together. There were always many German soldiers there, and they would laugh and joke

111

among themselves, just as British boys would do. When the lights were up during the interval, it was fascinating to look at them enjoying themselves, as I was, and to wonder why we should really be murdering one another. I remember one evening when a German corporal sitting next to me asked for a light. I told him I did not have one. He smiled sympathetically, and after getting a match from someone else thrust a cigarette on me. I thanked him profusely, and then spent an unhappy ten minutes smoking it. I am a non-smoker.

The doctor was busy not only in Resistance affairs; he had a large practice. Both morning and evening, during surgery hours, his waiting-room was full. Sometimes, late at night, there would be uniformed callers: German soldiers with VD. All German other ranks were issued with a card which was signed or stamped by the prostitute after *le bon moment* was over. The prostitutes were registered; so if there was an outbreak of VD reference to the cards of the men infected would reveal the probable source of infection. Woe betide any German who obtained his pleasure outside the happy circle. The flesh is weak, however, and when a young or old Teutonic brave sought experience elsewhere, and found to his dismay that all was not well below, he faced a court martial. His only recourse was private treatment from a French doctor.

Boury, and many other doctors, were in a position to exploit the situation as they pleased. Generally, they would refuse treatment, but occasionally, particularly if an officer was involved, they might offer help subject to certain conditions. These conditions always benefited the doctor or the Resistance. Indeed, the doctor told me how a Resistance group he knew of had brought a girl up from Paris for the sole purpose of giving VD to the local German commander, and had then blackmailed him to achieve their ends.

Of course, if a doctor was caught treating a German the consequences were serious, but risks were part of their existence. Some of the chances they took were incredible. Shortly before my arrival in Chauny, the doctor went to see an airman who had been shot down. His condition was critical, surgery was necessary to save his life. Boury and another doctor smuggled this sick airman into Chauny hospital one night and operated on him; they then smuggled him out again. There were German doctors and staff actually living in the hospital. I heard this story from Mlle Logeon; when I mentioned it to the Doctor, he was embarrassed.

'One day you will be suitably rewarded for that deed,' I said.

He smiled. 'I have been rewarded; the airman is alive and well.'

One of the doctor's friends was a prosperous farmer who kept open house for any airmen the Resistance wished to hide. He lived in the country, and the doctor had suggested to Bob that his house might be a good place from which to make our transmissions. The man was approached and said that he would be delighted to accommodate us; so one Friday morning we drove out to his house and worked the transmitter in his orchard. Our work over, he insisted we stay for lunch. We accepted his invitation and had an extraordinary meal. His wife, a pleasant middle-aged woman, appeared to be quite composed and normal when we had a pre-lunch drink, but once the meal began she wept continuously and ate nothing. Her husband and daughter took no notice of her, and conversed pleasantly with us as if nothing untoward was occurring. Both Bob and I were greatly puzzled, and when the farmer rose from the table at the end of the meal saying he was going to Chauny, the poor woman could contain herself no longer and, rising, left the room greatly distressed. 'You'd better go to her,' said the farmer to his daughter. 'I'll see you later.'

The girl left the room, and he turned to us: 'When I asked you to lunch I had forgotten today was Friday; I apologize for any embarrassment you may have felt.'

'Madame appears to be very distressed,' said Bob.

'Yes, yes; it is a long story. You see I have a friend in Chauny whom I visit on Friday afternoons and this upsets my wife. She is a very good woman and finds this friendship of mine difficult to understand. You are men of the world and you know what I mean. A man must live.'

Bob nodded understandingly. 'I was hoping we might come again, but perhaps it is not convenient?'

'My dear fellow, come whenever you want to. We must not let a woman's sensibilities interfere with the work of the Resistance.'

Bob, who was a pretty thick-skinned individual, took advantage of this last remark to explain why he was keen to return.

'What I should like to do is hide our equipment somewhere here and come every day for about a week. I do not expect we will have to transmit more than once a day so there is no danger of one of the radio-detection cars tracing us here.'

Our host, whom I will call M. Chevalier, indicated that he was not concerned, so Bob went on: 'We will keep a listening watch and get as much practice as we can, for with the invasion imminent it is vital that we prepare ourselves thoroughly.' M. Chevalier nodded, 'All of what you say is both understandable and acceptable to me. You are most welcome to stay as long as you like, but now,' he looked at his watch and hurriedly rose to his feet, 'I must be off; my friend is waiting for me. My daughter will help you find a hiding-place for your equipment; explain the position to her.'

As soon as he had gone Bob burst out laughing. 'Wicked old devil. Makes no secret of the fact even in front of his daughter.'

'You would think he might have more thought for his wife's feelings,' I said.

'What can he do?' Bob help up his hands. 'What can he do? She has discovered his secret and she protests. But what can he do? His wife is middle-aged and no longer as attractive as she was, he has a mistress who is, perhaps, young and attractive; must he give her up because his wife is upset?'

'Yes,' I said, 'for the sake of his marriage.'

'What do you mean, the sake of his marriage?' He looked puzzled.

'Suppose she left him?'

'That is unlikely, unless she has money of her own. A woman of her age needs the security of a home. She is too old to begin again. Besides, he treats her well and respects her; you heard what he said.' He rose and pushed his chair under the table. 'Come, we have work to do.'

Just as I got up, Mlle Chevalier came into the room. 'How is your mother?' I asked.

'She is quite well, thank you, monsieur; it is rather difficult to explain why she was crying. Perhaps my father ...'

'He explained everything, mademoiselle. Forgive my friend for mentioning the subject, but ...' Bob could not find words with which to finish the sentence he had started and stood gesticulating for a moment. It was the first time I had seen him at a loss for words.

'There is no need to apologize, monsieur; it is most kind of your friend to be so concerned.' She smiled sweetly and, turning to me, added. 'Do not be too upset, monsieur; my mother only cries on Fridays.'

The next few days were among the most pleasant I spent in France. Every morning I would leave the doctor's house and walk out of the town towards M. Chevalier's farm. Sooner or later Bob would arrive on his motor-bike and give me a lift. In this way no one saw us leave the town together. If anyone saw him stop and pick me up, that in itself could hardly matter. By leaving all the equipment in M. Chevalier's garden, we had greatly lessened the risk of detection when travelling. Without this equipment we had little to fear if stopped on the road, for our papers were in order.

Josephine Chevalier was a pretty girl of eighteen who had, apparently, inherited certain tendencies from her father. In her case they did not detract from a likeable personality, and I enjoyed her company very much. She would go out to the orchard with Bob and myself and showed great interest in our work. In the lulls between broadcasts, when Bob would wander over to the house in search of refreshment or to converse with Madame Chevalier, Josephine would remain with me. The reason she gave was that she wanted to practise her English, and my being there gave her unrivalled opportunities. Her mother, father and Bob apparently believed this, and so we saw quite a lot of each other. At first, it is true we did converse for long periods, but, gradually, as we got to know one another better, it seemed as if we had exhausted all conversation, yet I never remember being bored.

Madame Chevalier had a good sense of humour and both Bob and I used to pay her the most flattering compliments and tease her unmercifully but always in good part. Monsieur was out on his farm during the morning and often in the afternoon, and it was during his absence that the real jollifications took place. One afternoon, we played a gramophone and danced and were having a high old time when Monsieur came into the room. The sight of his wife dancing the Charleston with Bob clearly surprised him and I was sure this was the end of the party in more senses than one. He pretended to be amused, but the undercurrent of his emotions was revealed later when he reminded Bob that our week would be up on the morrow. Originally, Bob had had no intention of staying for more than a week, but I fancy he was as disappointed as I was at this virtual ultimatum.

Josephine and her mother were also disappointed and, when we left, Josephine whispered: 'If it is to be our last day together, come early.' I thought about her a lot that evening, and felt rather like a schoolboy who views the end of a good holiday and a return to work with equal disfavour.

We were out at the farm early the next morning and were met by M. Chevalier. After the usual pleasantries of the day he was brisk and very much to the point: 'Will you be ready to leave by lunch-time?'

'That depends,' said Bob. 'Why?'

'Because I have to go to Chauny this afternoon, and today being a day on which my wife is upset it might be best if we all left together.'

'Yes, today *is* Friday,' said Bob.

'Quite. You remember last Friday?'

'Very well. Madame was most distressed.'

'Exactly.'

'All right, we will try to finish this morning. The only thing is that we might receive a message requiring us to listen in later today.'

M. Chevalier nodded. 'I appreciate that if you must stay, you must, the Resistance comes first, but if possible I should like you to be ready to leave after lunch.'

We went to the orchard and switched on the set. 'Is there any chance that we might receive a message this morning?' I asked Bob.

He shook his head. 'Most unlikely.'

'Do you think Madame will be upset today?'

'Perhaps, but she has such a good sense of humour I can't understand her behaviour.'

'Well, he can't be all that easy to live with.'

'I agree, but her method is the wrong one for that man.' He got up. 'I think I'll have a word with her. Keep listening; see you later.'

No sooner had he gone than Josephine appeared. 'Oh, I thought he would never go; I must speak to you alone.'

She did not, in fact, have much to say, yet in her own fascinating way remained intensely interesting, and the thought that this was to be our last meeting, for the time being anyway, grieved me.

When we sat down for our pre-lunch drink, it became apparent that M. Chevalier was in a good humour. Whether this was because we were leaving, or simply that the afternoon's prospect was to his liking, I don't know, but he was most affable.

Madame Chevalier was charming, as indeed she had been the week before, when nothing she had said, or done, before lunch gave any indication of what was to follow. There seemed to be a glint in her eye, however, and occasionally she glanced at Bob in a knowing way.

Josephine had told me that her father had had his present mistress for two years, although her mother had found out only a year before. Ever since then she had put on her Friday lunch-time performance. It was her physical protest to what was in her eyes his licentious conduct.

We went in to lunch and sat down. Taking the lid off a soup tureen, Monsieur served generous helpings to all, including his wife. Then, turning to Bob he began discussing Resistance affairs. To my delight, Madame began drinking her soup and showed no signs of distress whatsoever. Josephine touched my foot with hers under the table and grinned down at her plate.

'I should like a little more soup, dear,' said Madame.

'More soup! Oh, yes, of course!' Monsieur took her plate and sank the ladle deep into the tureen, then stopped with a start and looked up. 'More soup! You have drunk your soup?'

'Yes, dear. Why, was I so very quick?'

'No, no, not at all.' He filled her plate slowly and handed it back, obviously flabbergasted.

'My word, this is good soup,' said Bob. 'Could I have some more?'

Monsieur took his plate as if in a dream and filled it, but made no attempt to hand it back.

'Could I have my plate?' Monsieur jumped, spilling soup on the table. 'Oh, I'm sorry,' said Bob, 'my fault.' Monsieur shook his head, presumably to indicate that he was to blame, picked up his own spoon and made as if to take some soup, then hesitated. 'Today is Friday, isn't it?' he asked.

'Yes, dear, this is the afternoon you go to Chauny.' Madame smiled sweetly at him. He put his spoon down on the table with a smack so that everyone looked in his direction.

'What is it, Daddy?' asked Josephine, now joining in the game.

'Nothing,' he said. 'I'm not hungry.' The plates were collected whilst he covered his confusion by whistling a little tune.

'No, dear, not at the table.'

'What?' he said.

'You were whistling.'

'I was whistling?'

'Yes, you were whistling,' said Bob. 'I was trying to think of the name of the tune. What was it?'

'What was what?'

'The tune you were whistling.'

'I wasn't whistling.'

'You were.'

'I wasn't,' he shouted, and banged the table. 'Come on, where is the meat?'

'In front of you, dear.' Madame was going from strength to strength.

'Oh, yes!' He looked rather stupidly at the small roast in front of him.

'You are lucky to get meat like this in occupied France,' he roared at me.

'I know,' I said. 'I'm very grateful.'

'You should be,' he muttered, and carved for every plate

save his own.

'Are you ill, dear?' asked Madame.

'Ill! Why?'

'You're not eating.'

'No, I'm not. I shall be visiting a friend in Chauny later and will eat then.' He spoke triumphantly.

'Oh, good, so long as you don't go hungry.' Madame spoke so pleasantly, without hate, rancour or sarcasm, that he could not retaliate. He sat there miserably watching us eat, too filled with remorse to say any more.

The meal over, the women left us with our coffee and went about their domestic chores.

'Come, Monsieur Chevalier,' said Bob, 'drink your coffee, you will be late for your appointment in Chauny.'

Monsieur looked up with tears in his eyes. 'All these years I have loved and respected my wife. Now I find she is a woman who can condone my having a mistress. How can a man be so wrong about a woman? How can he be so wrong?' He rose from the table leaving his coffee, and walked unsteadily to his study where he locked the door and remained for the rest of the afternoon. That was the last I saw of him; but Dr. Boury told me that he never visited Chauny on Friday afternoons again.

After my week in the country, town life seemed rather dull. Bob had gone off to Paris and had given no indication of when he might return, so there was no work for me to do. As a result time was rather heavy on my hands. The Bourys were charming and thoughtful hosts, and with all the comforts of their home at my disposal I had nothing to complain about. Indeed, I was never oblivious of my good fortune, for whereas most airmen in hiding had long and lonely days and nights to face, I had good company, books and a piano with which to while away the hours.

Yet, nevertheless, there was the frustration of waiting for something to happen, and never being sure what that something might be. Was I waiting for the invasion? For Bob's return? Or for some catastrophe such as would occur if the Bourys were betrayed? I never felt sure. And the subconscious strain of this doubt affected not only myself but everyone connected with Resistance affairs. The nagging uncertainty of what might happen; the nagging certainty of what would happen if the 'might' became reality, made life nearly unendurable for some, difficult for others, and hard for everyone. The sword of Damocles was over every head, and it is well to remember this when either criticizing or praising these brave people. In both the things they did and the things they left undone, the influence of this great uncertainty was always present.

Often I would sit by the window, just out of sight of passers-by, watching the world that was Chauny. Jacqueline would sit beside me and tell me who each person was, what they did, and all the whys and wherefores of the circumstances surrounding them.

'Do you see that man? He is a collaborator. It will be an unhappy day for him when the Allies arrive. And that woman? Her husband was shot as a hostage. That boy! He has no parents; his father was killed in 'forty, his mother is in a concentration camp.'

And so she would go on and on. Often the information was less dramatic than the instances I have cited, but there always was information, for these people were vital and animate with feelings, fears, hatreds, doubts, anxieties and hopes, influenced and affected by the difficult world they lived in.

The house across the road was occupied by a registered prostitute, and all day long uniformed clients flocked to her door. She did not receive them in the evening, the doctor's theory being that she had to get up sometime, and her best chance of doing so was when the German Army was sleeping. These callers, unlike the people with whom they rubbed shoulders, were unknown to Jacqueline, so no information was forthcoming. Yet in their own way they were equally interesting. Some would walk confidently to the door, and ring the bell with authority, others were more furtive: they would look this way, then that, perhaps light a cigarette, and adopt – with various degrees of success – an attitude of sublime indifference to the pleasures that awaited them on the other side of the door. Few of them remained inside for more than ten minutes. The more furtive an individual was before his entry, the quicker his re-emergence; only the very brazen remained for a quarter of an hour.

One day the doctor was expecting visitors, and asked me if I would like to go out for a couple of hours rather than be confined to my bedroom. I said I would, and shortly after lunch headed out of the town towards the country. Having been brought up in the country, it was no hardship for me to spend an afternoon among wild spring flowers, listening to the birds and observing Nature hard at work everywhere. I kept away from the main road and, after walking for about an hour, found a delightful spot on the edge of one of the many woods. I sat down and opened the book I had with me. The sun was warm and bright enough for me to screw up my eyes and alter my position slightly so as to make reading a little easier. Occasionally I would look up and view the green countryside before me and then consciously remind myself that there was a war on, and that not far from this peaceful scene men were planning each other's destruction. How futile it all seemed. How wasteful.

Slowly the sun moved on round the sky until its position told me that it would be safe to return to Chauny. On my way to the doctor's house I had to pass the railway station. On arriving there I was disturbed to find signs of great activity. The forecourt was crowded with German military trucks, soldiers and foreign workmen. French police were demanding the identity cards of all civilians who passed by and were already holding two men, presumably on suspicion. I had no wish to show my identity card, for although it was in order, this was clearly no ordinary check-up. Without really thinking what I was doing I walked straight into the centre of a group of foreign workmen and mingled with them.

'Who are you?' asked a big blond man who might have been a Norwegian. 'What do you want?'

Suddenly I found myself desperately short of breath and must have looked very frightened, for he changed his tone and asked kindly: 'What do you want?'

'Please help me,' I stammered; 'don't say anything to the police.'

His companions gathered round me curiously, much interested by my arrival.

'Don't crowd him,' hissed the big blond. 'Can't you see he

is in trouble? Don't attract attention to him.'

They re-formed their little groups, but too late, for a French gendarme was heading towards me.

'Your identity card, monsieur,' he demanded briskly.

'Certainly,' I said, trying desperately to look unconcerned. He scanned it for a moment.

'Why did you dodge into this group of men?'

'Dodge into this group!' I tried to sound incredulous, then had a sudden idea.

'I came over to see if there were any Yugoslavs here; I have not seen a compatriot of mine for a long time.'

'I had to tell him there are none in our party,' said the big blond.

The gendarme nodded, clearly convinced that I was speaking the truth, and handed me back my identity card.

'All right, but don't go away. Go and wait with those two men over there.' He indicated the two men I had supposed to be prisoners.

I nodded my thanks to the big blond, then walked over and joined the two men who stood by yet another gendarme who was quite obviously watching over them. None of us spoke. In no time our numbers had swollen to eleven; indeed, every able-bodied man who was questioned was eventually sent over to join us. Still no one spoke. A German officer came out of the station and our guards stood to attention. He was curt and to the point: 'I want you men to help us unload a train. You will be paid.'

He turned and walked into the station with eleven relieved men on his heels.

For some two hours we carried boxes of provisions and other stores and loaded them into the trucks outside the station. We worked alongside German troops, who in general ignored us. The other foreign workers were at the far end of the train so I had no chance of thanking them for not giving me away.

The unloading completed, we were formed up into a queue and filed past the German officer, who sat at a table and solemnly doled out a ten-franc note to each of us.

As I walked back to the doctor's house, I mused that I must be quite a rare specimen: not many British officers can have received pay from both sides during the war. And another thing: was I technically guilty of aiding the enemy?

Eight

It was the end of May, and of my fourth week with the Bourys. I was sitting in the lounge reading to Claudie, the three-year-old son of the local magistrate who lived next door, when Jacqueline came in with Mlle Logeon and Bob. I was pleased to see him and most anxious to hear what he had to say, but unfortunately, we had to wait until I had finished Claudie's story before the latter would leave the room. For some reason he had always called me Monsieur Canard, and did so when he left.

'What is this Monsieur Canard business?' said Bob.

'Oh, he always calls me that!'

'It is not a good name for a child to be shouting about; it sounds too much like a code name.'

'Ah,' I said, 'something must be in the wind for you to talk like that.'

'It is, René. The invasion is near.'

'Do you know when?'

'I don't know, but the point is that we need you to operate the radio.'

'Of course. When?'

'This afternoon. All the equipment is in the loft of Monsieur Logeon's garage. Now listen carefully: you are to arrive at 2.15 p.m. Don't use the front entrance, but come in through the garden at the back. You know where I mean?'

I nodded.

'We have a Frenchman with us now who can work the sets, but he cannot operate at your speed, and he makes mistakes. It is essential that someone takes down these messages accurately; that is why we have come back to you.'

It is nice to receive sincere flattery; rewarding to accept added responsibility.

I left the house after lunch and started to walk to the Logeon garage. On my way, I had to pass a crossroads in the centre of the town. To my concern, I saw large military cars parked on both sides of the road, and German and French police questioning passers-by. I could not turn back without arousing suspicion, so walked on. One of the Germans stopped me and asked for my identity card. I produced it in as unconcerned manner as possible and waited whilst he scanned it.

'What is your name?'

'Pierre Mehancio.'

'Your age?'

'Twenty-two.'

'Where were you born?'

'Zagreb.'

He handed the card back and bade me pass on.

By the time I'd reached the Logeon garage my pulse had more or less returned to normal, but it was soon stimulated when I saw the yard and garden was full of German soldiers. A truck had broken down and put into the garage for repairs. A sergeant and some men were working on the engine, and judging from the number of components lying about they would be there for most of the afternoon. The other men were lazing in the sun, obviously relieved to break the monotony of their journey. One or two nodded to me as I walked by, and nervous though I was the humour of the situation did not escape me. I entered the house through the open back door and was warmly welcomed by Madame Logeon and the others. I was glad to accept a glass of wine, and quickly related my recent experience. Their only reaction was amusement, and no sooner was my drink finished than Bob suggested we go upstairs and prepare the transmitter. It was so obvious from the way he spoke, and from the disinterested way in which Madame Logeon and the others went about their business, that the presence of German troops did not constitute a big enough menace, in Bob's opinion, to consider cancelling the transmission. I accordingly said nothing and followed him upstairs. All the equipment was in an attic and Bob had the transmitter aerial poking out of a skylight. He assured me no one could see it from the ground.

Fortunately, on this occasion it was a case of receiving messages rather than transmitting them. The transmitting station was powerful, and both its call sign and message came through clearly. It was necessary to transmit our acknowledgment several times before the operator heard it, which was no wonder with our aerial. Our procedure was to receive a message, acknowledge receipt, and then close down for a period for the message to be decoded. We would then start up again on a different frequency. The frequency and time of next transmission was given either in the message or just after its completion. By dodging from frequency to frequency the life of the German direction-finding cars was made more difficult and our job a little less hazardous.

There was great excitement when Bob decoded the message, for it inquired whether the local Maquis would be able to receive a supply of arms and equipment should it be dropped that night. Transport would be necessary, the message said, for some of the equipment would be heavy.

'We cannot take the lorry tonight,' said M. Logeon. 'We have no petrol, all my pumps are dry.'

Here indeed was a predicament.

Not being able to make any suggestions as to where they might get petrol, I sat back and watched their worried screwed-up faces as they racked their brains for a solution. There was M. Logeon, middle-aged, tough, sharp as a tack, wearing his garage overalls, more as a gesture to his profession than a necessity, sitting there with a furrowed brow betraying his concern; then his daughter, her pretty face disfigured by an angry scowl, rocking herself backwards and forwards on an upturned box. The young Frenchman who could operate the wireless paced up and down in the background; it had not been a good day for him. First, he had not been entrusted with the operation of the sets; secondly, Mlle Logeon seemed more interested in Bob than himself; and thirdly, he hadn't the faintest idea where petrol might be obtained. Every time he spoke M.

Logeon had something caustic to say, and now he felt like
a curate whose vicar will not let him take part in the
service. Bob sat there on another upturned box as
impassive as ever. He leant forward, elbows on his knees,
his hands cupped either side of his jaw, like a chess-player
considering the next move.

The minutes ticked by and at last I spoke: 'Shall I ask for
another hour?'

Bob nodded without speaking. I turned on the
generator; its hum, vibrating round the loft like an angry
bee, roused everyone slightly, and they watched as the
second hand of Bob's watch on the table approached the
zero hour. I transmitted the code group, and after a
minute the acknowledgment came back loud and clear: we
had another hour. I wondered what the operator in
England was doing. Did he understand what our
predicament might be?

'Of course those trucks downstairs must be full of
petrol.'

It was the young Frenchman who spoke.

'Do you suppose they might give us a few litres?' M.
Logeon's tone was sarcastic.

'They might. Could we not bribe one of them?'

'Wait a minute,' said Bob. 'We cannot bribe, but we
might use persuasion. Suppose we bring the Boche into
the house and give them lots to drink; they might become
amenable.'

M. Logeon considered the possibility for a moment or
two.

'We need girls. Jacqueline [this was his daughter's
name], see if you can find a friend or two. We must
persuade the Boche it is worth while to come in.'

She ran off downstairs, followed by Bob and the young
man.

M. Logeon turned to me: 'You will have to answer yes or
no within the hour. You had better stay up here
meanwhile.'

For some ten minutes nothing appeared to happen,
even the occasional noises from the yard where the
Germans were working diminished and then ceased.
Could it be that having completed their repairs they were

now leaving? If so, all Bob's plans would go awry. If they did would it matter so much? Would these arms make such a difference? In six months' time would they have affected the course of the war? These brave people were running fantastic risks downstairs; where was the man who could say these risks were justified?

My thoughts were interrupted by laughing, and shouting and the sound of happy people entering the house. They moved up the passage from the kitchen and, as they entered the parlour two floors below me, I might have believed myself eavesdropping on a private party. The sound of popping corks, girlish laughter and manly murmurings was so reminiscent of the mess on a ladies' night. People having a party make much the same noise anywhere. Presently someone began to play the piano, and a discordant version of 'Lilli Marlene' penetrated the floors below us. But time was passing and only ten minutes remained before I must answer yes or no.

A noise on the stairs sent me to the door, and there on the landing below was an inebriated Hun staggering about muttering to himself. How on earth had he escaped the attention of Bob and the others? This was really serious, for how was I to stop him entering the loft without using force? As I watched him the door of the parlour opened. I could not see it, but a sudden increase in the volume of noise, just as if someone had turned up the sound on a radio, told me what was happening. M. Logeon went down the passage with a German and into the kitchen. I ran back to the skylight and heard them walking in the yard; even above the din below there was no mistaking those steel-studded boots. Quickly returning to the door I found the German was now sitting on the stairs leading to the attic. He was not feeling well and appeared to be resting. For two or three minutes I watched him, praying he would not decide to come up. At last M. Logeon and the other German returned and entered the parlour. Almost immediately Bob came out, and running upstairs nearly fell over the sitting Hun. He pulled himself up with a jerk, and with great good sense sat down beside him. There was now less than two minutes to my deadline, and although I was sure Bob was running to me with good news, I dare not anticipate it and transmit in the affirmative. He coaxed the German to his feet and led him downstairs. I switched on the generator, at least the set would be ready. It was only a matter of seconds now. Bob had reached the ground floor and was leading the German up the passage. Time was now up. Something had to be done. I went to the set and began transmitting my call sign. It was acknowledged. They were ready to receive my message. What was I to do? I took a chance and using RAF procedure transmitted the 'wait one minute' signal. There was a pause, and I could imagine them saying, 'What's this!' then came the acknowledgment. A breathless Bob appeared at the door.

'The answer is yes,' he gasped. 'Make sure you get the time.' And then he was gone.

I transmitted the call sign again. The answer came back like lightning. I whipped out my code group for 'yes'. He acknowledged and sent his code group for the time. In my fear I had transmitted at top speed, and sensing the urgency of my signal he had responded. There is a language between wireless operators which the non-initiated can never know. He knew my situation was desperate, and I knew that he knew. When I sent my closing-down signal he answered, and then sent two pips. This was the unofficial and frowned-on greeting one RAF operator sent to another on signing off, so there was something else he knew as well.

That night the Logeon lorry went out and picked up a great quantity of arms which were subsequently put to good use by the Resistance.

I did not go out with the lorry, much as I wanted to, but was escorted home by a young French girl. M. Logeon felt it would be too dangerous for me to go home by the main road, so her task was to take me, after dark, by a round about route which culminated in the public gardens at the back of the doctor's house, where all I had to do was climb a wall and drop down into his garden.

All went well until we were only a few yards from this wall, when we ran into a curfew patrol. Their torches and German accents gave us just sufficient warning and we dived into the undergrowth. If they had been doing their job properly they would have seen us, but they ambled past chatting amiably and flashing their torches casually here and there without any apparent plan or purpose in mind. We lay quietly, side by side, neither of us speaking. The grass was wet with a heavy dew and I felt her shiver as the moisture seeped through her thin summer dress. I put my arm round her, more as a protective gesture than anything else; but she turned appreciatively towards me and kissed my cheek. This is madness, I thought, and made to rouse myself; but she clung to me and whispered: 'Don't move. We must stay until they have gone.'

'But they have gone, Mademoiselle.'

'No, it is a trick; they are probably near.'

I glanced down towards the direction in which they were walking and saw the flashing torch in the distance.

'I think they have gone, mademoiselle.'

'You talk too much, monsieur.'

'Yes, mademoiselle.'

'M. Logeon told me to look after you. I know what is best.'

I am not sure she correctly interpreted M. Logeon's meaning, but I didn't argue.

When I finally got home Jacqueline and the doctor were sitting up waiting for me. There was a pot of coffee on the fire and brandy on the table, further evidence – though none was needed – of their thoughtfulness and kindness. I gave an account of the days' happenings, culminating with our near squeak in the public gardens.

'But the German patrol went by nearly an hour ago; we heard them. Where have you been since then?' Jacqueline asked inquisitively.

'Since then? Oh, hiding in the undergrowth!'

'What, for an hour!'

'We had to be sure the Germans had gone.'

'You knew they had gone. They always go the same way.'

'I didn't know.'

'Well, Françoise knew!'

'I don't think she did.'

'Jacqueline,' said the doctor, 'don't question René so; they had a bad shock. Françoise was probably too frightened to go home alone straight away, and kept René with her until she was more composed. It is not pleasant for a young girl to be out alone in the curfew. Now go to bed; it is very late.'

Jacqueline nodded her assent and made to leave the room. 'Forgive me for questioning you, René. I am very tired and we were worried when you were so late.'

'Thank you for waiting up for me,' I said. 'It was sweet of you.'

'Don't mention it,' she smiled, and kissing her father left the room.

The doctor took my empty glass, filled it along with his own and handed it back. He rose and walked to the fireplace, eyed himself in the mirror for a moment, and then turned as if about to propose a toast. I looked up from my chair waiting for him to speak but he stood there pensive and silent, passing the glass back and forth beneath his nose. 'Little Françoise,' he said. 'I'd never have believed it.'

The invasion came a few days later, and though we were all expecting it, it was difficult to adjust one's mind to the fact that British and American troops were now fighting on French soil. The first news I received was on being awakened one morning by a loud banging on the back door. I heard Jacqueline run downstairs, and then the shrill high-pitched voice of the magistrate's wife shouting: 'Les Alliés ont débarqués.'

We spent the day huddled round the radio and, when it was announced that evening that bridgeheads had been established, our joy knew no bounds. Everyone seemed to think it was all over and that in a matter of days Allied troops would be in Chauny. When, as the days passed, it became obvious it was not going to be a quick affair reaction set in, and people seemed ridiculously depressed. The doctor had a secret room built under his surgery, and was sure he and his family would have to use it. Like many French people he feared the retreating Hun and his possible vindictiveness, yet, despite his fears, he operated on an RAF sergeant who was badly wounded in the groin, and attended the man every day until he was well again. Jacqueline and I used to visit him and try to cheer him up.

He suffered much, but bore his pain stoically. Indeed his principal worry was that the people who were hiding him were taking such risks. He knew he was too badly wounded to be moved and that any searching Germans must find him. He knew what the consequences would be for his helpers if they did.

It was while visiting him one day that I had one of my narrowest escapes from capture. I was walking down the street when the sound of an approaching aircraft made me look up. Only the previous day Jacqueline and I had spent an uncomfortable five minutes lying on our faces in the open, whilst Spitfires dive-bombed the canal. Some of the bombs had fallen very close to us, close enough for me to curse the inaccuracy of my compatriots, and to be more than ready to avoid a repeat performance. Anyway, so busy was I watching the sky that I stepped in front of a bicycle and a moment later was sitting on the road with a German corporal. Fortunately for me he had also been looking at the sky, and presumed he was to blame for the collision. He helped me to my feet and apologized in halting French for his carelessness, insisting it was all his fault. A crowd began to gather and I feared his concern for my welfare might have serious consequences, but, happily, the aircraft suddenly dive-bombed the canal and everyone scattered for shelter, allowing me to get away. A few days later, however, the doctor told me he felt it was now too dangerous for me to stay longer in Chauny, and that I would have to go into the country. The place he had chosen was a small farm near Marest, some ten kilometres from Chauny. I was sorry to have to go, but had been expecting something of the kind for some time.

I had only seen Bob once since that exciting day in the Logeon garage. We had gone out on his motor-bike and worked the transmitter in an orchard some miles out of the town, but without much success. He had told me that he was going away for a while and would not need me again until the Allied armies reached Paris. Unlike most people in Chauny, he appreciated that the invading armies had a tremendous task in front of them, and that it would be some time before he or I would enjoy the pleasures of freedom again.

The fact that he had no further use for me at the present time meant that there was no reason why I should not be in hiding in the country, as were all the other airmen hidden by M. Dromah's group. My presence in the town had been justified as long as the group could make use of me, but now, temporarily at least, I was as big a menace to their security as any of the other evadees. Indeed, Dromah considered me more of a menace. My knowledge of French and radio telegraphy had brought me into contact with most of the leaders in his organization and he was fearful lest I should be captured and tell all I knew. This was a problem I had to live with myself. The doctor always told me that they expected a captured member to speak eventually, but not for a day or two. 'If you are captured, remember every hour you delay telling them what you know increases our chance of escape.' What he said was very true, but I often wondered how one could endure the unspeakable tortures the Gestapo inflicted on their victims, without breaking down. I asked him what he thought the answer was. 'You need courage,' he said. 'The more you have, the longer you last; it's as simple as that. Some men die without revealing anything, others speak in five minutes. You can say much in defence of a man who breaks down under torture. You can cite circumstances, his physical condition, his sensitivity to pain, and so on, but the man who dies under torture or, if he does not die, never speaks, what can you say about him, or to him, or for him that is not in praise of courage.'

Nine

One evening I was sitting in my room reading when Dr Boury came in and told me there were two men in his study who wished to see me. 'They are perhaps British agents,' he said. When I expressed concern as to their authenticity he assured me that they had come by way of Dromah and their credentials were satisfactory.

I went down to his study to find two men, probably in their forties. One was tall and emaciated-looking with fair hair and eyes that appeared to look out from far inside his head. His skin had a yellowish hue and his clothes hung as if upon a skeleton. His companion, on the other hand, was stockily built with dark hair and the tanned skin of someone from the South – perhaps a Basque.

We exchanged the usual pleasantries in French and the doctor then left the room. As usual there were no introductions though it was accepted in a strange way that they knew who I was; but I would probably never know who they were.

The thin man bade me sit down and then speaking in English and without any recourse to small talk, indicated that he knew all there was to know about me. Where I was born, went to school, my squadron and details about my family. 'I have told you these things so that you will know I have the authority to give you orders.' His attitude was quite antagonistic.

I formed the opinion that excellent though his English was he was not British and wondered why he had reverted to my tongue unless he wanted me to think he was from British intelligence.

'We wish you to help us. The work may be dangerous so we will give you a gun.' He produced a revolver and gave it to me with a small packet of ammunition. 'You will be taken from here to Soisson where you will go to a house and ask for a certain person – you will be given a name later. You will give him this envelope – it will identify you.' He held up a small blue envelope. 'He needs you to work a transmitter. It is very important. Can we depend on you?'

'Of course,' I replied.

The two men then exchanged glances and the swarthy one spoke. 'If ever you are captured, tell them the truth, that you are a British officer. If they believe you there is a good chance they will not torture you – at least not straight away. I do not have to tell you that time will be everything for your friends here in Chauny. If they believe you are just an evading airman they will probably observe the usual conventions, particularly now that the Allies are in France.'

The thin man now took up the dialogue. 'You have been chosen for this mission for three reasons. The first is because you speak French and it is, therefore, much easier to move you about than other airmen; the second is because you can operate a radio transmitter and finally we know you are a person who will use a gun if necessary.'

'May I ask who told you that?'

They both smiled. 'Is it not true?' said the big man.

I hesitated, did this mean they knew Bob. 'It is true, I will if it is necessary.' My answer pleased them. 'Is it likely that I will have to use this gun?' I asked.

'It's for your own protection if you are cornered or run into difficulties.' The big man spoke in an almost offhand way.

'For my self-defence?' I was begging a question. Were they going to use me as an assassin?

His companion intervened, 'Or for your self-destruction.' He spoke dispassionately.

'After all,' said the fat man, 'in certain circumstances it could be an acceptable alternative. The Gestapo can be very heartless and unpleasant. You should remember this.'

They were inviting my suicide if anything went wrong sensing, quite rightly, the feelings I had for the Bourys and my other friends in Chauny to say nothing of my aversion to torture.

But why would they use me for anything if I were such a

potential threat to the local Resistance unless there was a very special reason? A full minute passed. I could not think of anything to say and they, experienced as they were, pressed home the point they had just made with their silence.

The thin man stood up. 'Have you any questions?' he asked.

I shook my head.

'Well then, I think we might ask the good doctor to join us.'

Dr Boury came in and was given a résumé of our conversation. Immediately he expressed his concern at the dangers of my being captured and the consequences that would follow; he was anything but convinced that the story they had told me to tell would impress the Gestapo. There was no giving way on their part, however, so he reluctantly accepted their assurance that I was required to make important transmissions. He agreed also that he would drive me, the following morning, to a farmhouse on the fringe of his practice.

After they had gone we went into the living-room where Jacqueline was waiting. We speculated as to whom these two men could be without coming to any firm conclusion. 'There are several secret agencies here in France,' said Jacqueline. 'The free French, that is de Gaulle's organization, the British, the American and then there are the communist cells in the Resistance and other splinter groups.'

'As long as they all work against the Boche,' said the doctor, 'so much the better. The trouble now is that politics is playing a greater part as our liberation draws nearer.'

'If only we could speak to Bob,' said Jacqueline, 'he knows so much more than we do.'

We all agreed but apparently Dromah knew that Bob was away for a few days and could not be contacted.

The next morning the doctor drove me to a farmhouse some miles out of Chauny on the road to Soisson. The farmer and his wife clearly were very nervous at accommodating an evading airman and I spent the day in a barn until the fat member of the previous evening's duo turned up with a lorry full of turnips and took me to yet another farmhouse a few miles from Soisson. His sinister accomplice was there and after supper with the farmer and his family we went into the front room where they briefed me further.

I was told I would make radio transmissions to England from a house in Soisson. The house was in effect a brothel. The owner, whom I will call M. Douamel, let three rooms to girls and otherwise shared the house with a Moroccan friend. There was an attic or boxroom at the top of the house and it would be from there I would operate. My first question was for how long. The Germans were constantly monitoring all transmissions and would certainly find a transmitter in the middle of a town in no time at all.

'Oh, only for perhaps two days and then you may return to your friends in Chauny.' As always, the thin man spoke with a note of irritation in his voice as if my questions annoyed him.

The next morning I travelled with the same load of turnips to Soisson and was dropped at a street corner near my destination. I felt abandoned and vulnerable for all there was to sustain me was the number of a house, a man's name, a blue envelope and a gun I hoped I would not have to use.

The house was gloomy and rather dilapidated like so many town houses after five years of war. I rang the bell. After perhaps a minute the door was opened by a short, plump man of very Gallic appearance with greying hair and a paunch depending for support on the buckle of the thick leather belt around his waist. He wore an open-necked shirt with the sleeves rolled up to his elbows.

'Monsieur Douamel?' I said.

'Yes,' he replied in English.

I concealed my surprise and continued speaking in French, 'I have a letter for you.' He took the envelope glanced at it and then, speaking in French, bade me enter.

The hall was larger than one would have expected from the house's exterior. It was not unlike the foyer of a cheap hotel though there was no reception desk. The doors to the four rooms that led off from it were all closed. He opened one and we walked into a large untidy office with a desk, some chairs and a table. He pointed to a chair inviting me to sit down. He opened the envelope then folded it inside out. There was no letter inside. He looked at me and smiled. 'So you are the British officer who has been working a transmitter for us.'

I was reluctant to reply to his question immediately for I was pondering the significance of his addressing me in English at the front door.

'You don't answer,' he raised his eyebrows and shoulders simultaneously as if mimicking a market stall-holder haggling over a price.

'I was wondering why you addressed me in English when we first met.'

He coloured noticeably. 'I – er – they did not tell me you spoke French,' he said rather lamely.

After an embarrassed silence we both dropped the matter, though such carelessness did not give me much confidence in my new mentor.

'The work you will have to do is dangerous. If the Gestapo come it is better not to be taken alive.'

Here we go again, I thought; always the suggestion that one must never be captured.

'But enough of this you will of course succeed. Come with me.' He pointed towards the door.

We rose and went outside into the hall. 'Up here,' he indicated the staircase. When we reached the landing a door opened then quickly closed. 'Ah, Monsieur, is shy,' he winked and gave me a knowing grin.

We climbed a second staircase to the third, apparently unoccupied floor. There was no covering on the stairs and our shoes thudded obtrusively on the squeaking floor-boards. We reached a landing much narrower than the one below. We went into a boxroom. Its contents were typical of an attic; broken chairs, various boxes, packing cases and a dilapidated bookcase. The solitary skylight was so filthy that only a limited amount of light could enter the room.

'Here, this chair is all right.' He gripped the back of an old armchair and pushed it towards me. So much stuffing was visible through what had once been leather that reason suggested it must be bug-infested.

'Where is the radio equipment?' My question appeared to surprise him.

'Oh, it will be here later. I must go now you will be quite safe here until I return.'

He went out closing the door behind him. There was a very audible click and then the sound of his feet hurrying across the landing and down the stairs.

I went quickly to the door. It was locked. The key was still in the keyhole.

What did all this mean? Why lock me in and leave the key so that anyone could unlock the door from the outside?

Why give me a gun and constantly refer to not being taken alive?

No, I was trapped. Why or for what purpose was completely unclear. What was clear, however, was that I must obey my instincts and get out of this place.

The door was too substantial to break down and my attempts to dislodge the key onto some old wallpaper I had pushed under it failed. To shoot out the lock was a possibility but would attract obvious attention and certainly bring the authorities to the house which for all I knew might be a genuine Resistance hideout. I heard footsteps and the voices of a man and a woman but did not dare to call for assistance since I had no idea who they might be.

It seemed unlikely that they posed any danger for they were both laughing. It was noticeable, however, that my attempts to hear what they were saying were hindered by the noise of the floorboards under my feet every time I moved. Some of them were very loose and this gave me an idea. If two or three of these boards could be prised up, perhaps the rafters were far enough apart to allow me to descend through the ceiling into the room below.

Using my service knife to cut away part of a floorboard, I made a hole large enough to enable me to put the leg of a broken chair into it with a view to prising it up. This turned out to be very difficult but persistence paid off and the board broke away. Unfortunately such was the force I had applied that the leg went through the ceiling causing a considerable amount of plaster to fall on the occupants in the room below.

I heard a man's startled voice demanding, 'What is happening?'

Unknown to me at the time, the couple whom I had heard arrive a little while before were sharing a bed to some purpose when half the ceiling had fallen on them.

The girl by virtue of her profession was probably not surprised by anything, but for the man this was obviously not the climax he had been expecting, 'It's a peeping Tom,' he shrieked. 'I will kill him, I will kill him.'

There was a pause, while presumably he put on some clothes and then the sound of feet pounding up the stairs. The door handle rattled. 'Open the door,' shouted the hysterical voice.

'It's locked on your side,' I called back. There was a surprised grunt and the door flew open. There stood a middle-aged man in trousers with braces hanging by his sides and a string vest partially covering an extremely hairy chest.

Before I could interest him in an explanation he shouted, 'peeping Tom' and aimed a kick at me. I dodged the first one but he came at me again kicking savagely. I caught his foot in the best unarmed combat fashion and held him standing on one leg. This did not improve his humour and he continued to hurl abuse at me.

'Monsieur, let me explain,' I began, but then thought, what the hell! Does he think I was locked in here to spy on him?

I twisted his leg round in the approved manner and as he went down thrust my right foot on his buttocks and pushed with all my might. He crashed into the bookcase and to my surprise his head went through one of the panels. He lay there stunned. I walked through the door shut it and locked it, taking the key with me. I walked down the stairs to see a young girl in a dressing-gown standing at the bottom.

'What have you done to him?' she asked.

'I tried to explain that I was not a "peeping tom" but he would not listen.'

'Have you hurt him?' she enquired in a matter of fact way.

'He is unconscious,' She smiled as if with satisfaction.

'I am a British airman.' I hoped this revelation might enlist her support and she reacted immediately.

'Did M. Douamel lock you in that room?'

'Yes,' I said.

She shook her head. 'This happened once before and men came back and took the man away. We think they were Gestapo. You must leave quickly.' She gestured excitedly.

I hurried down to the hall and carefully opened the front door. A car had drawn up outside with a uniformed driver. It appeared to be a German staff car.

Closing the door, I ran across the hall and into the room next to M. Douamel's office. I found myself in what could have been a doctor's waiting-room. There were chairs against the wall and a large table in the middle, covered in old magazines.

Voices in the hall sounded the arrival of Germans. There was some muttering and then the clatter of boots ascending the squeaking staircase. Before they could have reached the landing a furious banging started upstairs. My recent assailant had obviously regained consciousness and finding himself locked in was as resentful of his situation as I had been.

I opened the door a little and listened. From the top of the house an authoritative voice demanded in guttural French, 'Open the door.' The banging stopped. An absolutely hilarious exchange followed as an incredulous Frenchman, who was slowly recovering from the effects of concussion, attempted to tell a humorless German the story of how he happened to find himself in his present predicament.

The fact that the conversation was taking place through a locked door only added to the element of farce. The girl's voice could be heard from time to time as she tried to intervene but obviously to no avail.

Judging the moment had come to leave, I emerged from the waiting-room and found the kitchen and the back door. It was almost certain that there would be someone waiting at the front of the house, if only the driver of the car. Once seen my chances of escape would be remote.

Before I could open the back door a man appeared pushing a bicycle. He was the Moroccan the two agents had referred to. He opened the door and came in, regarding me with some surprise.

'Good day, Monsieur,' he said affably.

Before I could respond, he heard the sounds of the attempts to knock down the boxroom door and in a startled voice asked what was happening.

'There are some Germans upstairs trying to knock down a door,' I said.

'But why?' The look of surprise on his face truly suggested that he had no idea of what was going on.

Before I could answer his question the sound of someone else entering the hall forced me to conclude that the back door was now my only possible way of escape.

The Moroccan made as if to pass me and go into the hall. I did not give way effectively impeding his progress. 'What the ...!' he started to say and made as if to thrust me aside.

There was no time for explanations or arguments: I drew my gun. The effect was dramatic. He backed away from me, holding his extended hands in front of his face, as if to ward off my fire.

'Be quiet and I'll not hurt you,' I said. He nodded his compliance and dropped his arms. Whoever had entered the hall could be heard climbing the stairs. Was it M. Douamel?

Judging from the continuing commotion at the top of the house the boxroom door was more than equal to the Gestapo's efforts to open it, but open it they would so there was no time to waste.

I beckoned to him to open the door. This he did. There was a small backyard leading into an alley. 'You push the bicycle,' I said. We turned into the alley and walked towards what appeared to be a busy street. I had no plan but thought the bicycle might enable me to get away from this area of the town.

My immediate problem was how to get rid of the Moroccan or to stop him raising a hue and cry when I rode off. He solved the problem for me by suddenly thrusting the bicycle at me and then running into the busy street like a headless chicken.

There was a screeching of tyres and much shouting. I picked up the bicycle and went to the corner. The Moroccan lay face downward in the middle of the road and a crowd was gathering round him. Such traffic as there was had stopped. No one had eyes for me as I cycled in the opposite direction.

My first intention had been to use the bicycle only to get me out of the vicinity as quickly as possible but my confidence grew with the density of the traffic and I kept on cycling. Compared to Chauny, Soissons was a busy place and though cars were few, military trucks were in abundance as were German troups. On balance the ordinary soldiers posed no threat and were often friendly, something the Resistance exploited to the full.

There were no signposts, so once in the country my button compass was the only rough navigational aid I had. Fortunately I came upon some foreign workers who were waiting for transport to take them back to their billets and by enquiring where they were going not only obtained a lift to Coucy Le Château Auffrique but found myself on the main road to Chauny.

A warm welcome awaited me at the Bourys, but they reacted angrily when they heard my story and felt, with justification, that everyone known to the two agents was now at risk. The doctor went off to see Dromah and I sat down to my first meal since a cup of coffee that morning. At no time during the day had I felt any hunger but now, suddenly I was ravenous.

No sooner had I finished eating than Bob arrived with the news that we had to make a transmission right away. A plane was due to land later that night with ammunition and supplies for the Resistance; we had to transmit vital navigational information concerning the rendezvous. Bob had the radio equipment with him so straight away we went upstairs and made the transmission.

While we were transmitting the doctor returned with Dromah who was aware of the pending arrival of the plane later that night though not personally involved. Because of the long light evenings we had to wait until nearly midnight before we could leave the house for the rendezvous, so I had plenty of time to tell Bob of my adventure. He was furious, not only because of my treatment, but because these two agents had taken me away without his knowledge and he demanded to know why Dromah had let it happen.

'If René had not returned this evening there would not have been anyone available to make the transmission. What would we have done then?'

Dromah defended himself by saying that Bob had told him he would be away for several days and he had not known anything of the 'drop' that was to take place that night until only an hour ago.

Dromah then took Bob aside and they talked earnestly for some minutes. I learnt later that he had been explaining why he had had to accommodate the two agents. His reasons certainly satisfied Bob but neither the doctor nor I were ever privy to them.

Later we went out, under cover of darkness and cycled behind the doctor's car to a wood some ten miles away where we joined a Resistance group. If the doctor was stopped, we would have time to dismount and take to the fields, or so Bob said. To me it seemed too simple by far and unnecessary for we were going only to watch the arrival and departure of the plane or so I thought.

I knew the collection was being organized by the group we were joining but was surprised when the 'look-out', who challenged us, asked 'Is this the airman?'

More men appeared and went into a huddle with Bob and the doctor. There were glances in my direction and I wondered if my presence was welcome. However, after a minute or two they came over to meet me. I was greeted cordially and taken through a wood to a small clearing where a landing-strip had been prepared.

Shortly a Lysander arrived and touched down between the fairy lights. Apart from arms and an assortment of packages a man got out and was hurried away without speaking to any of us. I turned to Bob, 'Is anyone going back in his place?'

'No,' he replied and then, fully appreciative of the reason for my enquiry, he murmured, 'I am sorry, René. It is not possible, you are not important enough. We have asked.'

A man I assumed to be the group leader then came up and took my two hands in his and expressed his regrets. I turned to Bob, 'So this is why we came.'

He nodded. 'I was hoping to give you a pleasant surprise.'

I watched the plane taxi away and take off down our improvised flare path. A few hours earlier my thoughts had been concentrated on survival; then I had experienced the elation of a successful escape. Now, as my transport to freedom soared into the sky, a black cloud of depression descended over me. During the last twenty-four hours my stamina had been tried and tested to the full, but now I had to call upon hidden reserves to keep my composure, as I walked back to my stolen bicycle through the muttered condolences of men who understood.

Ten

The next day Jacqueline and I cycled to a farmhouse near the village of Marest which was to be my place of recuperation and reflection for the next month. As we pushed our bicycles up the short path from the road to the farm I saw it was built in the shape of a quadrangle. The small house, two barns and other farm buildings forming three sides, a high wall across the front, the fourth. There was a door in this wall and you had to pass through it to reach the house. An old-fashioned bell hung there and it clanged solemnly when Jacqueline pulled the chain attached to it. The door was unbolted and opened to reveal a plumpish good-natured woman of perhaps fifty, who embraced Jacqueline and bade us enter. This good lady was a clairvoyant, and her clients came from far and wide. She was married, and her husband, a kind little man, paid much attention to what she had to say and helped her run the farm. Their principal source of income was Madame's precognitive power; but the farm was still important and they ran it efficiently.

A few days after my arrival in Marest Bob came to the farmhouse and gave me an explanation of what he believed my abortive mission was meant to accomplish. The Resistance in the Soisson area were having a difficult time with the local Gestapo Chief and wanted to dispose of him. It was almost impossible for the Resistance to kill a German because up to fifty hostages were shot after any such killing as a reprisal.

On the other hand, the Germans were so pedantic that if the execution were carried out by an Allied airman it was believed that the question of reprisals would not arise, particularly if the Allied airman died as well.

Enquiries were made and I was chosen as the most likely candidate. The problem was that because I spoke French and had travelled about the area I knew too much about the local Resistance and its members for them to risk my being captured. Bob admitted that unwittingly he had provided information about me, particularly our pact that we would not be taken alive. He thought they had wanted to borrow me to work a transmitter and knew nothing of the assassination plot.

Bob believed Douamel was a double agent working for the Allies. The plan finally agreed upon was for me to be delivered to Douamel and for him to advise the Gestapo that a British airman had come to him for assistance and that this airman was hiding in his attic.

The local Gestapo chief was very much a 'field' man who made a point of making arrests himself. When he opened the door he would have been a framed target at short range. Although armed he would not expect an evading airman to have a gun. The hope was that he would be killed before the back-up squad killed me. For the plan to work my death was essential; if I survived and spoke under torture the Chauny Resistance group would be betrayed as would others who had helped me.

Bob admitted that he had told them he did not think I would let the Gestapo take me alive if I were armed. This, no doubt, was the reason for the constant reference to suicide when I was being recruited. How much Bob knew for certain is a matter for conjecture; I was never able to contact him after the war. When I did learn of his true identity he had died.

My first week passed quickly and pleasantly. My quarters were comfortable, the food good, the house clean, and I could wander about without any risk, so long as I stayed within the quadrangle. Every afternoon, Jacqueline came to visit me, bringing news, books and her engaging personality. We would sit in the yard or, when a client came, in one of the barns. Unfortunately this happy state of affairs was not allowed to continue, for Madame, quite rightly, said such frequent visits might arouse the suspicions of her neighbours and clients. Jacqueline was to come only once a week. Deprived of company in the afternoons – Monsieur was out in the fields whilst Madame awaited her clients – I began to take an interest in the animals and their behaviour. What a revolting lot they were! The chickens fought and squabbled and ate their young, and once pulled a small duck to pieces when it cut itself on some glass. One mother rabbit ate her litter as they were born, and the goat stank to high heaven. The reason for this was, I found by observation, that he urinated through his beard. He appeared oblivious of the stench beneath his nostrils: I was not. Monsieur had a dog, a sort of retriever, who spent most of his time hunting rats. When he killed one he would keep it in his kennel until his master appeared, when he would lay it at his feet and receive a reward. These rats were a real menace and often killed small chickens at night.

Another scene which was quite new to me was the execution of farm animals by Madame. The rabbits she would hold up by their feet and smash their skulls with a heavy stick; the chickens and ducks had their heads cut off with a pair of scissors whilst Monsieur held them. When the killing was in progress, all the other chickens or rabbits, as the case might be, were in a state of panic, but once the unfortunate creature was dead they all settled down again as if appreciating it would be a few days before Madame would come out in search of another victim.

Madame was very proud of her powers of clairvoyancy, and would impress on me how dependent her clients were on her skill. I wanted to ask her how long it would be before the Allied armies reached this part of France, but never did so. Every evening we would listen to the radio and hear good news from the Russian front, but there seemed virtual stalemate on the invasion front.

'Why don't they advance?' she would ask me. I often wondered why she could not answer the question herself, but her crystal remained under the cloth on the table, reserving its advance information for the paying customers.

The days became weeks and I sensed that I had outstayed my welcome. Not that they were other than nice to me, but the strain was telling on Monsieur, and he insisted that I spend all day in the barn. Since the weather was very hot, and the barn very stuffy, my days were uncomfortable.

Towards the end of July, I had a birthday. Jacqueline arranged for her visiting day to coincide with this event, and came with a cake and presents. I was touched by her kindness and we had a happy picnic in the barn. Madame killed a chicken that afternoon and she and her husband entertained me in the evening. I had wondered why they had not joined Jacqueline and myself for tea, but learnt from Monsieur – after he had drunk a little too much – that they considered us lovers who preferred to be alone. Feeling Jacqueline's honour was at stake, I assured him – as was perfectly true – that there was nothing between us. At first he looked at me in astonishment, but later, when I had repeated my statement several times, with disdain.

'You, the son of a Frenchwoman, spend afternoon after afternoon alone with a girl in a barn, and then admit nothing has occurred between you; you should be ashamed of yourself.'

The way he put it, I almost was.

The news from the Western Front improved and, just after my birthday on the 25th, the Americans captured Avranches and thus opened the way for General Patton's army to begin its great advance across northern France. The Resistance was now very active, and the news bulletins gave instances of how the Maquis were harrying the retreating Germans and helping the Allies. Between 2 and 10 August, Dinan, Rennes, Mayenne, Le Mans, Nantes and Angers fell in quick succession and, intoxicated as we were by this splended run of successes, we never attached the importance we should have done to the Panzer attack the Germans launched in an attempt to recapture Avranches on 7 August. If this attack had succeeded, Patton's army would have been cut off, but during the vital period, 7 to 12 August, our conversation centred on when Paris would be liberated, not whether the Germans might recapture Avranches. In the end, it was the Germans who were cut off and destroyed in the area of Falaise, nicknamed the 'killing ground', so complete was their destruction. The local police had apparently obtained control of Paris, most of the German forces having left, but as yet no Allied troops had formally entered the city.

New invasion forces landed between Marseilles and Toulon, and everywhere, or so we gathered from the news bulletin, French Resistance forces were distinguishing themselves.

Although the news delighted my host and hostess, it also made them more and more nervous. Many German troops were about in the area and some had called at the farm and tried to buy food. I knew they wanted me to go, although nothing was said, and I intended to do so, but badly wanted advice from Jacqueline before setting out for the Allied armies. She would be able to tell me where to make for, and perhaps know of a hiding-place in the woods near Chauny should I be unable to penetrate the German lines.

Accordingly, I asked Madame if I could stay until Jacqueline returned, promising meanwhile that I would leave immediately should anything untoward occur. Madame agreed, but at once sent for Jacqueline, who arrived breathless on her bicycle with the news that the roads were crowded with German troops. Madame insisted that I leave at once and, after all she and her husband had done for me, there was nothing I could do but agree. But Jacqueline would not let me just wander off, and insisted that I take her bicycle and go to the doctor's house in Chauny. I argued, but her point that it would be ridiculous to be caught now, after six months of evading capture, when Allied troops were only a couple of hundred kilometres away, made sense, and I reluctantly agreed to do as she said. She would walk back – she had nothing to fear from the German convoys – but a man of my age on foot might be thought suspicious, on a bicycle less so. This was her reasoning, and although embarrassed at taking her only form of transport, I knew better than to argue.

My ride to Chauny was a nerve-racking experience. The bicycle was much too small, forcing me to cycle with my knees turned out rather in the manner of Charlie Chaplin. The first Germans I came on had been machine-gunned from the air and were busy getting a truck out of the ditch. They paused in their labours and watched me cycle by. I was sure they were going to stop me, but they had more on their minds than a foreign worker on a bicycle. As I neared Chauny, the sound of aeroplane engines quickly followed by machine-gun fire and exploding bombs added yet another hazard to my journey. 'What next?' I thought, and slowed down so as to give the planes time to finish their work, but the convoy I had passed through earlier was now back on the road and thundered up behind me.

What happened next, I'm not quite sure, but I was in the ditch with my bicycle while tracer bullets whined off the road and hard-revving trucks thundered by to a chorus of shouting from frightened Germans. I have a faint recollection of seeing a Spitfire coming up the road towards me. He appeared to come silently, for the first truck behind me with its attendant noisy convoy drowned all other sound. I believe I saw him rock his wings as he adjusted his aim. A twitch of the handlebars, a dive, and I was out of his sights, flat on my face in the ditch. Even then, I don't think I was quick enough. It was just that no bullets hit me.

The attack was over in a flash and the convoy went on, so after a minute or two I resumed my journey. The Spitfire showed no sign of returning, but even if he did the convoy, which was now miles away, would be his target, not me. There was a good deal of aerial activity, however, ranging from the steady droning of high-flying aircraft to the angry buzz of hedge-hopping fighters. Each time one of these fast little beasts zoomed by like an enraged hornet, I was mentally in the cockpit with the pilot. What did he think of the rather dull flat countryside beneath him? Would he be fully conscious of his ability to terrify and destroy? Did he identify his victims as men possessed of personalities and feelings or were they merely 'the enemy', an abstract problem to be dealt with coldly and impersonally? When it is a case of kill or be killed and the enemy is a live presence, heat and passion play their part, indeed without them many would fail; for fear can make a man hate, and hate make him kill. But when shooting up a convoy the dice are too heavily loaded for the pretence that 'kill or be killed' enters into it. There is some risk, it is true, from small-arms fire, but with height, speed and fire-power at your command you are master of the situation.

When on a bombing raid, despite, the provocation we felt at being shot at by anti-aircraft guns and enemy fighters, I never remember feeling other than sad when we dropped our bombs. The thought of the death and destruction they must cause sickened me. I remembered our very first operation, when we had got lost and flown over Switzerland, bombing Stuttgart an hour late and alone. The sight of the blazing town below appalled us as a crew, yet Jack made two runs before he dropped our bombs. We received rough handling from the AA defences and were very glad to leave, but crew discipline was excellent and, when Ernie called up every member on quitting the target area, but a slight alteration in the pitch of some voices betrayed the concern we had all felt. 'Two thousand years of Christianity and this is the best way men can settle an argument!' It was Ernie who spoke, but it summed up my feelings exactly.

Just outside Chauny, I had to pass more German troops encamped on the edge of the town. Again I attracted attention but no one stopped me. On reaching the doctor's house, I attempted no deception but parked the bicycle and rang the front-door bell as if a patient. Unfortunately, more machine-gunning started down by the railway, and it was some time before the door was opened by a frightened maid who told me the doctor was out and that I would have to return later. She would not allow me to wait, despite my protestations that I was sick, on the grounds that the doctor's evening surgery did not begin for three hours. Fortunately, Madame Boury was at home, and hearing us arguing, came to the door. She had the good sense to intervene by asking what the trouble was and then gave me permission to await the doctor's return. The maid, with some reluctance, showed me into the waiting-room and there I sat until Madame dispatched her on an errand.

'Where is Jacqueline?' demanded Madame Boury.

'She is walking here,' I said sheepishly, and began to explain what had occurred. To my great concern Madame became nearly hysterical and nothing I could do would console her.

'I did only what I thought best, madame.'

'Yes,' she cried, 'what was best for you. Why could you not think of that poor girl out there on the road in all that fighting?'

'There is little risk, madame, they are only attacking the convoys.'

'Yes, and if she is there when a convoy is attacked?'

'All right, madame, I will go and find her and give her the bicycle. I am sorry it has worked out this way, but I did only what Jacqueline thought was best.'

'No, you must not do that, there are too many Germans about; if you are captured on her bicycle we may all perish.'

Frankly, I did not know what to do, so just sat there while Madame cried, asking myself if my behaviour was as bad as she made it out to be. I was confident Jacqueline's assessment of the situation had been accurate and that she had known what was best. As she had pointed out, there was a good chance that a cyclist would get through unmolested, whereas a pedestrian would be forced into conversation by curious locals and possibly be questioned by German troops.

The doctor's return was the signal for a further display of anguish by Madame. I was really sorry for her, but at a loss to understand why she was so distraught. In the ordinary way, Jacqueline would not have returned until evening, and the bombing and machine-gunning had been going on for some time without it being thought necessary to confine her to the house. No! Madame was worn out by years of occupation and worry and now, with the prospect of freedom within a few days, was plagued by an anxiety neurosis that nothing should happen to spoil everything at the last moment. I was to know exactly how she felt a few days later. The doctor quietened her and gave her a sedative, declaring confidently that there was nothing to worry about. But it was obvious he was concerned, and I felt angry and ashamed that I had given way to Jacqueline's pleadings and taken the wretched bicycle.

'Where do you think she will be by now?' asked the doctor.

'I don't know,' I said. 'How long should it take her from Marest?'

'About an hour.'

'Then if she left when I think she did she will be here soon.'

He nodded. 'Nevertheless, I'll take the car and go out to meet her.' But before he left the room, Madame began crying hysterically: 'Oh, my poor little one, my little girl, you are alive!'

We turned and saw a tired-looking Jacqueline passing the window. Both mother and father rushed to the front door, leaving me alone and disconsolate in the living-room.

Supper began in a strained atmosphere but ended happily. At first Madame Boury was still angry with me for having taken the bicycle, Jacqueline was tired, and the doctor worried.

'It is too dangerous for you to be seen here. The Germans are very vicious at the moment and would think nothing of shooting us all on the spot, if they found you. We must hide you until I can contact Dromah. I believe there is some talk of all the hidden airmen taking to the woods, but we shall see. Meanwhile, you will have to spend your days in my secret hiding-place.'

I thanked the doctor for his offer, but after my experiences of that afternoon had decided the time had come for me to fend for myself and that I must move on. They would have none of it and insisted that I remain a few days longer.

'If you leave now, I will reproach myself for evermore,' said Madame Boury. When it appeared that even she wanted me to stay, I agreed to remain for a few days; principally to enable the local Resistance chiefs to decide whether I, or any other evadees, might be of use to them in the fighting that was, we felt sure, to follow.

My next few days were tedious in the extreme. Every morning, after an early breakfast, the carpet in the doctor's surgery was rolled back, the linoleum taken up, and a flush-fitting trapdoor revealed. This trapdoor gave access to a small cellar-like room in which was placed a deckchair. There was a tiny grille in the side of the house through which some air filtered, also a little light, but not enough to enable me to read. Apart from giving me an unrivalled opportunity for meditation, there was little to commend my hiding-place. I had my thermos flask and sandwiches, and for an hour in the morning and evening there was the doctor's surgery above me, with talk of aches and pains and tonics and 'Isn't the news wonderful, Doctor!' Apart from this, however, only outside noises such as diving fighters, machine-gun fire and bombs helped the time along. Not that I was depressed. The news was too good for that. The day of liberation was near: so near in fact, that all kinds of possibilities passed through my mind, as if to show me how easily things could still go wrong for us all.

Every evening, his surgery over, the doctor would open the trapdoor, and I would come up and join them for supper. I slept on a couch near my hiding-place, ready to go down should anything happen.

On the morning of what was, I think, my eighth day, I was alarmed to hear footsteps above, and the sound of the carpet and linoleum being moved. The trapdoor opened and Bob's face appeared. 'You poor old devil,' he said. 'Come up and let's have a look at you.'

I climbed out, and saw that Jacqueline Logeon was with him, also Jacqueline Boury and her mother.

'You don't look too well. Are you feeling all right?'

There was a slight note of anxiety in his voice so I guessed he had work for me to do.

'I'm fine, but after a week down here a little fresh air would be pleasant.'

He laughed: 'Oh, you'll get plenty of fresh air from now on! We need you.'

'What for?'

'Well, the Americans will be here soon. In a few days' time and there will be a procession of retreating Germans. We must make life as unpleasant for them as we can. We shall also be using the transmitter.'

'If they're retreating, wouldn't it be better just to let them go? If you start attacking them, they'll merely take reprisals on the local population.'

'He is right,' said Madame Boury. 'They are revengeful.'

Bob flushed with anger.

'The Americans need our help. It is our duty to make war

on the Boche in every possible way.'

'I agree,' said Jacqueline Boury, 'but isn't it sensible to be discreet?'

'Killing Germans is the most sensible thing I know,' he retorted. 'Now the moment has come to fight, everyone has reasons for not fighting.'

'Perhaps they are good reasons,' said Madame Boury tentatively.

'Good reasons!' he said scornfully. 'Selfish reasons is more like it. Everyone is afraid.'

'They have good reason to be afraid. The Germans are capable of anything.' Madame spoke soberly, and in my opinion made good sense, but Bob wanted not merely justice to be done, he wanted it to be seen to be done; and, in his case, seeing meant being in at the kill. His attitude was understandable after all he and his countrymen had endured; but, with the greatest respect, I feel it showed a lack of consideration for others, who would be unable to fend for themselves as the Maquis could. It would be a case once again of the aged and feeble, the women and children unwittingly suffering consequences brought about by the actions of others.

The doctor returned home just before we left, with the news that Paris would fall at any moment.

'I have just seen Dromah; he is very confident it will be today. Allied troops are waiting to move in.'

When I said goodbye, we thought it was only for a few days.

'As soon as we are liberated, come straight back here,' said the doctor. 'We'll have such a party!'

In fact, it was two years before I saw them again, but that was not my fault.

Bob and I cycled off towards the small town of St Gobain, where, I gathered, we would be operating against the Germans when they arrived. We stopped at a farmhouse on the way for Bob to discuss something with a Resistance member, and were greeted with the news that Paris had been liberated. For some reason, this news meant that Bob had to return to Chauny immediately, so it was arranged that I spend the night with his friend and that he would pick me up the following morning. All that afternoon and evening the radio blared out the good news: 'Paris est libéré.' The house filled with happy men and women, special bottles of wine appeared, chickens were killed, and we had a party. My host was clearly delighted to have an Allied airman in his home, and boasted of the fact to every new arrival. Why so many people came to this particular farmhouse I don't know, but come they did.

The radio played continuously and, every five minutes, or so it seemed to me, a dramatic voice declared: 'Paris est libéré.' Every time this announcement was made, it was greeted with acclamation. My host's son, a man of my own age, seemed quieter and more sober than the others and I felt I could ask him what would happen if any Germans arrived.

'Oh, we're taking it in turns to keep watch; there's always someone down by the road to warn us of approaching danger. Indeed, it will shortly be my turn.'

'May I come with you?' I asked. 'I should like some fresh air.'

'Of course; we will go now if you like.'

We wandered down to the road and relieved the sentry, who was only too pleased to get back to the party.

For a little while, we sat in silence, listening for suspicious sounds but hearing only the jollification behind us.

At last he spoke: 'I shall be glad when it is all over.'

'Won't we all,' I replied.

'Not all, I'm afraid. There will be many who will be sorry, even if they don't know it yet.'

'What do you mean?'

'I mean,' he said, speaking quietly and coldly, 'the party will soon be over, and not all the guests will want to go home.'

'The party?'

'You must forgive me, I was drawing an analogy. The noise behind me, you know.'

'You mean there are people who want the Germans to stay in France?'

'No, not exactly. I mean there are people who, because of the peculiar circumstances existing in France today, are very important. When all this fighting is over, they will have to go back to their farms or their desks; they will not longer be important. They will have to accept the highest wage or salary a prospective employer will offer them. When it is not very high, they will not like it. There are many such men in France.'

'What will you do when it is all over?' I was curious to hear his answer.

'Oh, I hope to go to the Sorbonne. I want to be a lawyer.'

'Is that your father's wish?'

'He's not really my father; he has looked after me since my parents were killed in the retreat of 1940. He would like me to be a farmer, but I have no great love of the land. I want to live in a world of ideas and discussion, not of turnips and milking cows.'

The following morning, Bob returned and we cycled to St Gobain. We lunched at the home of a friend of his where Bob had established his headquarters, for want of a better name. It was rather like a robbers' lair, filled with grim, determined men, all armed to the teeth and apparently thirsting for blood. It had been Bob's intention I should stay there, but I overheard his friend's wife protest that my accent was too foreign and she would rather I slept elsewhere. Accordingly, I was taken to another house just outside the town and spent the night there. My arrival was somewhat inopportune, for the daughter of the house was in the throes of childbirth. The baby safely delivered, however, my new friends made me very welcome.

After supper, I was introduced to the mother and babe and allowed to join in the merry-making the happy event occasioned. Two parties on the trot was more than my abstemious constitution could stomach, however; and, after a bowl of coffee the following morning. I took a walk with the son of the house, hoping to dispel my hangover.

As we wandered through the woods near the house I asked him, more to make conversation than for any other reason, where his brother-in-law was.

'He's in hiding. It is not safe for him to stay at home; the Germans are looking for him.'

'Then it is much too dangerous for you to hide me; the Germans might come at any time.'

'Not at all,' he said. 'They would recognize him, but they don't know you.'

The incongruity of this statement left me at a loss for words. 'Only an Irishman could answer that one,' I thought.

There was a sound of diving aircraft overhead and looking up we saw an American Lightning fighter engaging a Messerschmitt 109. Within a minute the sky was full of aircraft: Lightnings and Messerschmitts. We climbed a convenient tree right on the edge of the wood and from this grandstand viewed the most incredible spectacle I had ever seen. Planes dived and twisted, engines with full boost applied roared their defiance at one another, machine-guns chattered. It was like watching goldfish in a bowl on a shelf above you, darting one way, then another, as if without design or purpose. But there were both design and purpose, for suddenly, with engine shrieking as if in pain, a plane fell from the sky, dark smoke billowing behind it. Out of this smoke came a small white ball and a swinging figure descended as the parachute opened. Another plane fell the same way, then another, but no parachutes appeared. The ground shook when they struck and fires burnt at three points of the compass. Then a Messerschmitt was blazing like a fireball but still flying on a straight course with two Lightnings spitting behind it. The pilot jumped; his parachute opened; but his clothes were burning, and the flames licked up above him to his lifeline, and he fell faster and faster, a streaking incandescent glow till, like a meteorite, he was extinguished. We looked up again and saw a 109 losing height rapidly as it flew away towards the north-east. The fight moved on, but one more plane spiralled down near the horizon and disappeared as if it had missed the edge of the world, pilot and parachute following at a more leisurely pace. The remainder passed out of sight.

We clung to the tree in silence, listening for any sound, watching for any sign of their return. The youth touched my arm and pointed. A cow with swinging udder and inflated stomach ran slowly across the field in front of us, mooing fearfully in pain and terror. I watched the wretched animal as she crashed her way through the small hedge separating one field from the next, and then plunged into the wood in desperate search of shelter. She paused panting, and bending her front legs lowered her head to the ground, then rolled exhausted on her side. But her rest was short-lived, for the sound of aircraft engines filled the air again and with a loud bellow the poor creature struggled to her feet and, protesting bitterly, moved farther into the wood. The triumphant Lightnings passed overhead, a good mission accomplished.

We climbed down and walked slowly back towards the house. My companion was silent and thoughtful, as well he might be: not many people had ever witnessed such a spectacle. Fighter aircraft normally fought at high altitude, too high for anyone on the ground to see or appreciate what was going on. To witness such a dog-fight, only a few thousand feet up, was an almost unique experience. Then there had been the horrible sight of the burning man and parachute, to say nothing of some half-dozen crashing aircraft, and the awareness that a man had died in most of them. No. It had been a fantastic performance, but a chilling experience; the thought of those burned and broken bodies sobered any sense of exhilaration one might have felt.

'It was an incredible sight,' I said, more to start a conversation than for any other reason.

'It was,' he agreed.

We walked on a little farther and came on his father and another man, both looking anxious and worried.

'You saw what happened?' said his father.

'I'm afraid so,' he replied, and then turning to the other man said: 'I'm so sorry.'

The latter shrugged his shoulders.

'It's war, but what do you think will happen?'

'Oh, the calf will die, and perhaps the cow too.'

I said nothing, but followed the three unhappy men back to the house.

Eleven

I spent the afternoon with Bob and some of his friends, prowling about in the woods. They seemed to be a trigger-happy bunch and I was fearful of what they might decide to do. Not that I had anything against harrying or sabotaging the German lines of communication or even fighting them outright if something concrete could be achieved thereby. What I did not want to see happen was for these fellows to do something purely for the sake of doing something, and then to see the local population annihilated by a revengeful German commander. This had happened before and could happen again. If the American advance was to continue, as it was doing, and the Germans went on retreating in orderly fashion, leaving the civilian population alone, why do anything to upset this highly satisfactory state of affairs? If, on the other hand, the advance should be checked, or some American patrol find itself in difficulties, then I was in favour of our giving them support in every possible way. I made my views known to Bob: he was passively unimpressed. This determination to fight the Boche which I had seen them demonstrate everywhere made their behaviour in 1940 all the harder to understand.

I spent quite a lot of time listening-in on certain frequencies but no one sent us a message, a fact which irritated Bob greatly. The news bulletins were of necessity sketchy and, of course, at least a day behind the advance. Without definite information to act on Bob wisely restrained the wilder elements in our party from showing their hand too soon. In many ways this lack of information probably saved a good many French lives; and, of course, some German.

The following morning I had two surprises: the first was the sight of the mother of only two days doing the family wash, even if aided by her mother. The second was the arrival of Bob on a bicycle, followed by some twenty Frenchmen similarly mounted. The son of the house immediately produced two more bicycles and we all rode off. After a couple of miles or so we dismounted and wheeled our bikes into the wood. I soon saw what was afoot, for Bob and the others took up positions from which they could watch a German convoy wending its way up a hill on the other side of the wood. Bob called me over.

'The position is this, René: the Germans are using this road to move back supplies they do not want to leave behind. They are forced to use any transport they can lay their hands on; they are even using horse-drawn vehicles. What we must do is wait until a straggler gets separated from the main party and then pounce.'

'Will the supplies they are moving be much use to you? I mean it might be a cartload of blankets.'

A look of exasperation came over his face.

'What is the matter with you? Don't you want to fight?'

'Yes, Bob, I'm as ready to fight as anyone, but why risk the lives of everyone in St Gobain for the sake of a cartload of blankets?'

'Don't listen to him, Bob,' said one of our party. 'If we carry on as he suggests the Americans will be here before we have time to do anything.'

'Wouldn't that be a good thing?' I interjected. 'Surely all you want is to be liberated?'

'Be a good chap and leave things to us,' said Bob. 'If we were not sure this was the right thing to do, we wouldn't be here. We want to serve our country and this is the only way we can do something positive.'

'So long as we kill a few Germans we must be helping France,' said the man who had previously spoken. Everyone nodded in assent.

'I'm only thinking of the women and children in St Gobain,' I said. 'If I'd been afraid to fight I'd never have got here in the first place, please remember that.'

'I did not mean you were afraid,' said Bob. 'It's your trying to tell us what to do irritated me. We know the risks, but we're prepared to take them to kill a few Germans, and the people are behind us.'

'All right,' I said. 'You and I have worked together before, Bob. You know you can depend on me. I'll help in every way I can.'

'I know that, René.' He held out his hand and we shook. This gesture evidently appealed to the others, for I subsequently shook hands with all of them and, mutual confidence restored, we went back to the war.

For a long time the only Germans to pass did so in convoys of at least six vehicles, all moving fairly briskly, so no attack was possible. We did not have a rifle between us, but most of the party had automatics and one or two of them, large revolvers. Bob insisted, however, that in so far as it was possible there was to be no shooting; we did not want to attract attention, for there were too many Germans about. The plan was to overthrow the driver and any guards there might be quickly and silently and drive the horse and cart into the woods. I had asked as casually as I could what would happen to the Germans, and learnt that they would be executed.

'We will cut their throats, or a very good method is to put a man's head against a tree trunk and strike the other side with a rifle butt.' Bob spoke casually, and, misinterpreting the look on my face, went on: 'I can see you're wondering what rifle butt. Every German has a rifle with him and we'll use his own.'

'It's a pity that we have to kill them quickly and silently,' said the man lying next to me as we watched the road. 'I'd make it slow and long if I had my way.'

For the first time the true impact of what an execution meant became a reality. 'It is worse than war,' I thought, 'much worse.' I had seen cities burning; people brought out of crashed and burnt planes and from bombed buildings; had dropped bombs, even had them dropped on me, and had accepted it all as war. But now I was to see a man executed in cold blood, primarily because my companions wanted it, and secondly because there was nothing else they could do with prisoners save kill them. Yet this, I reasoned, is better than civil execution. These men are killing out of revenge, hate and for reasons of security. It is wrong, morally and ethically, but understandable. On the other hand, take the execution of a murderer, justified though it may be. His executioners (by that I mean all those involved in his execution) perform their allotted civil tasks without rancour, without hate, but with a loathing and repugnance all decent men must feel. They execute him, not, we are told, so much as a punishment for his crime, but as a deterrent to others. Thus society protects itself, and pays men to perform the odious task of killing a fellow being, and believes it has found a solution because not one-tenth of one per cent of the people know what is involved. If they did, another answer would have to be found.

Then a horse and cart came into view and began slowly climbing the hill. I watched, horrified, as it neared us, knowing too well that I had no stomach for the task at hand.

Bob was issuing instructions, but I heard him as if in a dream. We moved to positions nearer the road and waited. The horse was making heavy weather of the hill and it seemed as if it would never reach us. The German got down from the cart and took the horse's bridle, exhorting it to greater effort. He was a man of at least sixty, tired and rather dishevelled. His walk was heavy and laboured, his air dispirited; but his weary voice had a kindly tone as he sympathetically urged the horse on. It was to no avail, however; the animal was exhausted and could go no farther. They both stopped. He considered the animal for a moment, and then laughing to himself and shaking his head walked back and put blocks behind the cart wheels. Our party was thrown into confusion: if the animal had walked another twenty or thirty yards, they would have had the German before he'd known what was happening. When he had dismounted my companions had smiled with satisfaction at the way fate was playing into our hands. But this was a setback. Bob signalled to us to go deeper into the wood, meaning to get round behind the man and his cart. But twenty men cannot move through bracken without making a noise, and hearing noises ahead of him the German grabbed his rifle and looked about suspiciously. Everyone froze where they were and the only sound was the snap of his breech-block as he charged his barrel. This was the one thing Bob had not wanted to happen: the man was ready to shoot it out and we dared not fire. Bob motioned to us to go farther into the wood, which we did, making a good deal of noise. A rather high-pitched German voice demanded who was there, but got no answer. After we had gone a couple of hundred yards, everyone gathered round for a council of war.

'We can't attack him now,' said one man, 'unless we shoot him, and that's too dangerous.'

'Suppose some of us distract his attention while the others get round behind him; we might do something that way,' said another.

It was quickly agreed that this was the best plan and we deployed accordingly.

I was with the party that was to do the distracting, and returning to our former positions we made what were meant to be distracting noises whilst Bob and the others were moving round behind our prospective victim. The German repeatedly demanded who was there without getting an answer, until at last, exasperated, he left the cart, and rifle in hand marched up the road to investigate. All we could do was beat a hasty retreat lest he start shooting. Unable to see anything from the road – he was too sensible to leave it – he turned round and walked back to the cart. Unfortunately, this was the moment Bob and his party chose to emerge from the undergrowth only to find the German facing them. There was nothing they could do except keep walking, while the now very nervous soldier covered them with his rifle. He said nothing, and they passed him without incident. But now the horse, as if determined to reduce the situation to bathos, followed the thwarted Maquis members to the top of the hill, where the driver climbed into the cart and trotted past the would-be assassins. The German was puzzled, but so were the French.

We cycled back to St Gobain, a quiet and somewhat chastened company. It seemed to me that either my companions were devoid of a sense of humour or that my own was perverted. True, I had not wanted to kill the old man and they had, and the outcome was not, therefore, tragic from my point of view, though it might be from theirs. However, I am sure twenty Britons would have reacted differently to such a situation.

Several German vehicles passed us on the road and an officer in a staff car eyed us most suspiciously. It was extraordinary to me that these Frenchmen who were so careful and security-minded dared monopolize the highway so blatantly.

All through the afternoon retreating Germans passed through the town and I was tempted to set off in search of the American spearhead. The only thing that restrained me was the fact that I felt it was my duty to stay and help Bob if he could use me. Since apparently no one wanted or needed to send us messages, I spent a lot of time listening to news bulletins, in the hope of being able to pass on any official information as soon as it was released. The information was, of course, out of date by the time we received it, but it did allow one to mark up a map and review the position as it had been say twenty-four hours before.

It was while I was thus occupied that evening that I found myself first in a most frightening and then a most embarrassing situation. My map marked up to date, I was sitting in the loft of Bob's HQ listening to some fine music I had just tuned in and wondering what it was, when there was an awful crunch and the house shook terribly. I pulled off my earphones, switched off the set, and ran downstairs and out into the street. The air vibrated to the sound of four-engined bombers, and the whistle of falling bombs mingled with the cries of frightened people as they ran for the air-raid shelter near at hand. I was about to run with them, when I saw some German troops stop their truck and crowd into the shelter with the locals. It would probably have been quite safe to join them, but I was too frightened to do so when it became apparent that the shelter was full and there was some friction between the oppressors and the oppressed. I ran into a field and lay down behind a tree only to have a bomb land within fifty yards of me. The force of the explosion and the vibration of the ground lifted me off my stomach and dropped me on my back. For what seemed an eternity earth fell like rain, while all I could do was to hold my hands over my face and ward off the spiteful shower. At last it stopped, and I turned on my face, spitting and coughing, half aware that another salvo was falling at the farther end of the town. No sooner had the echo of the exploding bombs died away than there was a sound I had often heard during the London blitz: it was as if an enormous lorry were tipping a load of bricks into a gravel pit, and it told me that a house was falling to the ground. In terms of time, the whole attack was probably over in two disastrous minutes. Disastrous, because the American Fortresses had apparently bombed St Gobain in error and achieved nothing save the destruction of innocent Frenchmen's property. My friends were just as annoyed as the other inhabitants of the town, but had the advantage over them in that they could vent their sarcasm on me, and this they did to some effect. There was nothing I could say in mitigation of what had taken place. You cannot explain the difficulties of target identification to people who have never flown, or the possibility of navigational errors to people who know nothing of navigation. The fact remained that the Americans had bombed St Gobain; the French wanted to know why, and I could not tell them. One of the elder men was particularly unpleasant, following me about for most of the evening crying: 'Ce n'est pas un travail, ça!' He was quite right, of course, but also old enough to know the consequences of war are as illogical as war itself. To the best of my knowledge no one was killed, though people were hurt and several houses completely destroyed.

By the following morning the roads were so full of retreating Germans that any thought of attacking them was out of the question. I saw Bob briefly, after breakfast, and attempted to transmit a message for him but was unable to get through. He was desperate for information and went off to make contact with another Maquis group, hoping they might be better informed. I spent the day with the son of the house in which I was staying, watching the retreat, and counting the Allied formations passing overhead. Nearly every formation came back exactly as it had gone out, thus implying that they were completing their missions almost unopposed. Towards evening we returned to St Gobain to see if Bob had returned with any information. He was not yet back, but an excited youth told us that the Americans were in Septvaux a few miles down the road. At first, I could not believe this, for there were still plenty of Germans in St Gobain, and they did not look as if they were expecting to fight in the near future, but the youth insisted and produced a packet of Camels to substantiate his story. I was thunderstruck.

'Who gave you those?' we both asked at once.

'An American,' he said. 'They're giving them to everyone.'

'How long ago was this?'

'Half an hour. I've just got back.'

'Why did you come back?'

'To tell my mother and father. They would give me only one packet of cigarettes, so my parents will have to go back to get more.'

'But how did you get through the German lines?'

'There are no lines, people are just cycling down the road to meet them.'

'Then why don't the Americans come on to St Gobain?'

He shrugged his shoulders.

'I don't know, perhaps they're waiting for supplies!'

I turned to my companion.

'What on earth does all this mean? If the Americans are just down the road, why are the Boche so unconcerned?'

He shook his head in wonderment.

'Can it be they don't know?'

'That may well be the answer. If it is, we had better get down there as soon as possible before they find out what's going on and close the road.'

'Mind you,' he said confidently, 'we could still get there over the fields.'

'Why make an easy task difficult?'

He nodded in agreement and we mounted our bicycles. Before riding off, I thanked the boy for his information, and then as an afterthought asked:

'Did any of the Americans speak French?'

'Not a word, that's why I had to come back. They could not understand that the extra packets of cigarettes I wanted were for my parents.'

I laughed. 'How could you think of cigarettes at a time like that?'

'Like what?'

He was puzzled.

'Well, you had just met your liberators after all these years; wasn't that enough without cigarettes?'

'I don't understand you,' he said. 'After all we've been through the least they can do is give us some cigarettes.'

We cycled to the outskirts of the town to find a German platoon, deployed as if to defend the road. We stopped and dismounted, as did some Frenchmen coming up behind us, uncertain what to do next. I was not particularly worried about our safety, for there were plenty of local people about and it was no crime to ride a bicycle. It was merely that my feeling that the happenings of the last fifteen minutes were too good to be true had, apparently, some substance.

'We'll have to go by the fields,' I whispered to my friend.

He nodded. 'It looks like it, but let's wait and see what the others do; some of them are men from Septvaux and they'll want to go home.'

I eyed them hopefully as their numbers grew. They muttered among themselves, too preoccupied to take any notice of us. 'Good news travels fast,' I thought. They were all arguing with an elderly man who had made some suggestion. After a moment, he cycled past us and up to the NCO in charge of the platoon. They talked for a moment or two, and then the old man turned and waved his companions on. Without saying a word we cycled down the road in the midst of them and through the German soldiers.

For a while, I restrained my exuberance; but once the Germans were out of sight I could contain myself no longer and, putting my head down, pedalled madly past all the Frenchmen in front of me. My companion hung on close behind and we were soon well ahead of the main party.

All the old man had done was to say to the NCO that we

wanted to return to our homes and had he any objection. The German had thought for a moment and then said he had none. Whether the Germans knew how near the Americans were, I don't know; subsequent events suggested they did not. All I know is that nothing during the period I was evading capture has mystified me more than the ease with which I passed through the German lines and to the American.

We rounded a corner and there was the village below us. As we descended the hill, I saw guns covering us from a high bank on our right and signalled my companion to slow down. A couple of Americans were standing at the side of the road a little farther down the hill, holding tommy-guns which they kept trained on us until we stopped.

'Just another couple of peasants,' said one to the other.

'That's where you're wrong,' I said. 'I'm an RAF man.'

'Gee, ain't that great, he speaks English! The captain will be pleased.'

'Of course I speak English, I'm an RAF man.'

They both looked puzzled.

'Royal Air Force! I'm a British airman. I was shot down seven months ago.'

'You're British!' yelled one of them. 'Yeh, I know, British Air Force. Gee, ain't that great!'

They both clasped my hand with such sincerity and good-will that the fact they had never heard of the RAF seemed forgivable.

The arrival of the rest of our party kept them occupied for a few minutes, but once they had passed them through they called up an NCO who took me into the village to meet the captain. The preliminaries over, the latter, a tall athletic fellow of about thirty regarded me affably.

'Well, Scott! I guess you must have had quite a time these past months.'

I agreed that was so.

'Well, now you've got a chance to do something useful at last. I need an interpreter.'

'I'll be only too pleased to help, but I must get back to England as soon as possible.' I was quite emphatic.

'Yes, sure, in a day or two, but meanwhile I can use you.'

'I was hoping to start for home right away.'

'Sure, we all want to go home, but there's work to be done, and you can help me to do it.'

'But it's my duty to return to my unit as soon as possible.'

'And so you will, as soon as possible. Meanwhile I'll fix you up with a uniform.'

'A uniform?'

'Yeh, you don't want to fall into Jerry's hands dressed like that. They'd shoot you as soon as look at you.'

'That's a chance I've taken for seven months; a couple more days won't make much difference.'

'It will, boy,' he said, stretching back in his chair. 'You're with a fighting unit now; anything can happen.'

'Meaning?'

'Meaning, we've got no lines of communication half the time. We're advancing so fast we keep outstripping our supplies. We might be surrounded at any minute.'

'I see. Is that why you can't pass me back down the line?'

'It's one of the reasons.'

'There are others?'

'Oh, sure!'

'What are they?'

'Well now!' He scratched his nose and grinned. 'Let's just say there are reasons.'

'But I'd like to know what they are. I don't want to be a nuisance, but after seven months here it would be nice to go home.'

'Home,' he said pensively. 'Yes, home's a good place.' He took out a gold cigarette case, opened it and passed it over to me. I declined for the second time in five minutes.

'Oh, yes, I forgot; you don't.'

He took one himself, closed the case, tapped the cigarette vigorously on it, put the case away in his breast pocket, and produced a lighter, also gold. He paused reflectively before lighting up.

'Home, that's the place to be; haven't been home for eighteen months myself.'

'Well,' I said, somewhat abashed, 'that's not exactly what I meant.'

He grinned wickedly and lit his cigarette.

'No, of course you don't. I know what you mean. For

seven months you've been giving the Krauts the slip, and you've had enough of it. Now you see a chance of getting right away from them and you want to take it. I'd feel the same myself.'

I brightened up a bit.

'Then you can understand why I wondered what your reasons were?'

'Oh, sure.'

I waited for him to go on, but he remained silent, puffing his cigarette contentedly.

I tried again.

'These reasons, are they confidential?'

'No, they're not confidential.'

'I see.'

'Do you?'

'No.'

He threw back his head and laughed: 'My, oh my! You're a character; you English are so polite.'

'And patient,' I added.

He chuckled, and shook his head at what was to him inexorable persistence, and then went on: 'The truth of the matter is you're just not important enough. If you were some general or something, I'd send you back in a jeep with an escort, but you're not. The colonel would want to know what I was up to if I pulled some of my boys out of the line to escort you back to HQ. You'll just have to come along with us until a truck comes up from base or we have one going back.'

'Couldn't I go back alone?'

'You could try, but the way things are moving you'll be a lot safer if you stick around here.'

'You're sure I won't be in the way?'

I spoke in a tone, half sarcastic, half suggestive that I was not asking for favours.

He was quite unabashed, however. 'No, you'll not be in the way. We'd soon tell you if you were.'

He rose, indicating that our interview was at an end, and called his sergeant.

'Fix our friend here up with a uniform and let him have K rations; he's on the strength for the next few days.'

The latter nodded, and we made to leave the room, but

the captain called after us: 'Mind your language, Bill; he's an English officer and a gentleman.'

We edged our way past the villagers who crowded round the sentry at the entrance, the hearty bellow from within following us out into the street.

'A great guy,' said the sergeant; 'always good for a laugh.'

My room-mate from St Gobain was waiting for me in the street and immediately plied me with questions concerning the Americans' future movements. I could not, of course, tell him anything, and he was most disappointed.

'What are you going to do tonight?' he asked me.

'Oh, they've taken me on their strength. I shall sleep here with them, or we may be moving on. I don't know.'

He looked worried. 'What about your bicycle and the things you've left in my bedroom?'

'Oh, you can have all my personal effects. There's not much there, but you are welcome to what there is.'

'Do you really mean that?' he asked excitedly.

'Yes, of course. It's little enough after what you've done for me, but the bicycle is more difficult. Do you know anyone you could leave it with here?'

'Don't worry about it, I'll take it back with me this evening. I can manage two bicycles and it's not far.'

'But the Germans are still in St Gobain. Wouldn't it be better if you stayed here?'

'I've nowhere to sleep here. I'll go home. Besides, my mother and father will want to know what's going on.'

I felt uneasy at his returning to St Gobain but could not dissuade him. We parted, believing we should meet on the morrow, and I went off with the sergeant.

The personal effects in question consisted largely of articles of clothing I had collected since arriving in France. They were of little value really, so I was glad that someone could use them and be pleased to do so.

The sergeant was not, in fact, able to give me a uniform, supplies not being available in the village. He gave me a helmet, however, with a second lieutenant's gold bar painted on it and a waterproof jacket. Everywhere the villagers were doing their best to fraternize with the Americans, offering them wine, and receiving in return cigarettes, chocolate and so on.

The troops, it seemed to me, were embarrassed by the attentions they were receiving and rather fed up at the way their rations were solicited. I did not see a single American under the influence of drink; they were a well-disciplined, serious body of men, who understood their popularity and enjoyed it, but never forgot the war.

I was attached to the unit guarding the approach to the village from St Gobain and spent the night in the open. It rained heavily, giving me first-hand experience of what infantry endure as a matter of course. I could have returned to the village to sleep, and the sergeant in charge suggested that I did so, quite rightly pointing out that there was no reason why I should get wet. But a stubborn pride made me sleep shivering under a groundsheet. I wanted to do a turn of duty during the night, and the sergeant said he would call me, but he never did. When I remonstrated with him the next morning, he just laughed and said he had forgotten.

I awoke, cold and stiff, just as dawn was breaking. The rain had stopped; but there were pools of water everywhere. I walked over to the sentries nearest to me, who were, as it happened, the two I had met on my arrival the previous afternoon. We exchanged expletives and viewed the dismal landscape together. Our position was that nearest to the road, so when the early-morning calm was disturbed by the sound of a motor approaching from the direction of St Gobain, we were instantly on the alert. The vehicle stopped just before it came into view and we could hear its occupants speaking German. Although the bank we were sitting on was well above the road it was not high enough for us to see round the bend ahead.

'They're Germans!' I whispered. Both my companions stiffened.

'Are you sure?' one of them asked.

'Of course I'm sure.'

They both brought their tommy-guns to the ready. Looking to my left, I saw the sergeant and others moving round behind us. No one spoke. The Germans were chatting away quite unconcernedly in what appeared to be a three-cornered conversation. The engine started again and an open amphibious car came slowly into view. The grey uniforms of the three occupants confirmed their nationality. The Americans waited till the car was level with us, then jumped to their feet and fired down at the three men. The Germans were taken completely by surprise, but retaliated strongly and fired back. Bullets whined over my head as I lay there watching, but the Americans stood their ground, firing continuously. The car accelerated furiously, but the increase in its engine's revolutions was matched by the additional fire-power it encountered from every side, culminating in a crescendo of shouting in the middle of the village.

Within minutes an American lieutenant arrived in a jeep demanding an explanation. A patrol moved up the road to investigate and reinforcements arrived and deployed.

I went back to the village with the lieutenant and found the captain standing by the German car. A dead Wehrmacht officer lay at the side of the road, his badly wounded NCO beside him. The driver, who had come through the ordeal unscathed, stood with his back to a wall, an American holding a tommy-gun a few inches from his stomach.

'How bad is he?' said the captain to a medical orderly who was attending to the NCO.

'Pretty bad, sir; he needs hospital treatment as soon as possible.'

The latter nodded and turned to me.

'Hello, Scott, been taking a bath?'

'A bath?' I said, puzzled.

'You're kinda wet.'

'It rained all night.'

'I know, but how come you had to be out?'

I explained.

'What are you trying to prove?'

'Nothing. I was attached to a unit; I stayed with them.'

He made a face at the lieutenant and went on: 'Well, look! We've got a blood wagon and an ambulance coming up; you can have a lift back in one of them. Meanwhile stick around.'

He walked off with the lieutenant, leaving me looking down on the wounded man. The medical orderly spoke: 'I guess that's all I can do for him. The poor guy keeps trying to say something. Do you speak German?' I shook my head, rather touched at his concern for the enemy.

The villagers were beginning to gather round the two prostrate figures, and as soon as the medical orderly turned his back they descended on them and began to ransack their pockets. I ordered them back and they left the wounded man, but others continued to search the dead officer for valuables. Other Americans soon appeared and the villagers made off, glaring angrily at me, not without some loot. I did not know any of them personally, and they were not sure who or what I was. Only my friend from St Gobain had known I was not French, the others who had arrived with us had probably not noticed me, and the locals had been too busy fraternizing to pay any attention to new arrivals. The wounded German looked pleadingly at me and spoke. I could not understand a word, and feeling self-conscious in front of the staring villagers, pretended not to be aware that he was addressing me. But he kept on and on, the tone of his voice becoming more and more desperate.

'The poor guy really wants us to know something,' said the medical orderly. 'Can't you make out a word?'

'Not a word,' I said, kneeling down beside the man. 'Is he in great pain?'

'Probably. He's got a lot of lead in him, and he don't look too good to me. If that ambulance takes much longer it'll be a wasted trip.'

Again the German tried, his desperate, pleading eyes bulging. I spoke to him in French and English, but he understood neither. Suddenly his head dropped back and a look of sheer despair crossed his face. He closed his eyes and muttered what might have been a prayer, then opened them and stared uncomprehendingly at us. The American looked at me and shook his head. He lifted the German's hand and felt his pulse. The eyes became glassy and the mouth slowly opened till the face held a lunatic expression, and I realized that he was dead.

'We tried,' said the American. 'The poor guy was just too far gone.'

I got up and walked across to the bullet-spattered car, took a German greatcoat and threw it to the orderly, who covered the body and then crossed himself.

I walked away from the two bodies and sat down to await the ambulance and my lift back to HQ.

The remaining German still stood against the wall, but was now smoking a cigarette which a well-meaning American had given him, to the intense annoyance of the French men and women who were watching. The captain returned with his second-in-command and surveyed the two motionless bodies. 'Dead, eh!' he commented, and came over to me.

'For Pete's sake haven't you got a dry uniform yet?'

'No, I'll have to wait until I get farther back down the line. They've nothing here. I'm still waiting for transport.'

He nodded and walked over towards the German, who took the cigarette out of his mouth and stood to attention. 'Has this guy been searched?' he asked.

'We made him turn out his pockets. There's his stuff over there, sir,' said the soldier holding the gun.

'Well, frisk him properly; he may have something hidden away, I don't like the look of him; he's shifty.'

A corporal ran his hands over the German and produced a small bomb. The captain smiled sardonically. 'Maybe that'll teach you a lesson, soldier; don't trust a Kraut another time.'

The soldier made a gesture of annoyance and threatened the German with his gun. The latter, thinking he was about to be shot, cried out in terror and held his hands protectively in front of him.

'Steady, soldier! Remember he's a prisoner of war.'

The captain's tone was emphatic and the soldier relaxed.

While all eyes had been on the German, several small children had run out and removed what they could from the body of the NCO. They were quickly chased away, but not empty-handed. The 'blood wagon' arrived and removed the bodies. When the driver opened the rear doors, two rows of stretchers were revealed, arranged in shelves one above the other. He slid the two Germans into place for their last journey in company with two Americans and a Frenchman. Five pairs of boots were all that was visible from outside the wagon.

Twelve

The 'blood wagon' did not give me a lift back and I was not sorry. The reason was an order changing the direction of the advance. Instead of going on to St Gobain, in effect we retreated along the route up which the Americans had advanced on the previous day, before they had turned off in another direction.

I rode in a troop carrier with new companions, who made me welcome and treated me with exaggerated respect. I had entered their carrier on orders from the captain. In the hurry and bustle of moving off he had given me no explanation, and in the circumstances it did not seem politic to seek one. In fact he chose this carrier because its occupants, having lost one of their members in battle two days previously, had room for me.

My feelings were very mixed. I had thought the previous evening that my worries were over, that a day or two would see me home. Now, far from retreating homeward, I was advancing towards Germany. It was not fear of battle that disturbed me; indeed, had I still been with the Maquis, I would have accepted the prospect of a fight as inevitable and necessary. There would have been the feeling that one must earn one's freedom. Freedom, in my case, temporary though it might be, had come almost too easily, though it was none the less welcome. When I had reached the American lines my feeling was that I had successfully – thanks to my French friends – evaded capture. Now, I might not only be recaptured, but killed! One episode in my life had ended successfully, only to be followed immediately by another. I was learning a truth: incidents can only be separated in retrospect.

At last I got a uniform. It came from the kit of the man

who had been killed, and was quite new and unworn. This uniform had an amazing effect on my morale. I felt suddenly not only warm and comfortable, but able to look any man straight in the eye again. For seven months, not only had I worn labourer's overalls, but had contrived also to look as inconspicuous as possible. Whenever a stranger had addressed me, my reply had been mumbled, my demeanour subservient. In the presence of Germans, a slouching walk and a dispirited air had been adopted. Even when talking to the captain, I had felt ill at ease, so scruffy was my appearance. Now I was a man among men again, and the feeling was wonderful.

We retreated to what was, I believe, the village of Prémontre, and then advanced to the north-east through Suzy, Cessières, Molinchart, Cerny, and so on, by-passing to the west Laon, which had fallen the previous day. No one seemed to know where we were going. An order would be given to advance up a particular road and we would advance. This was very different from the RAF, where the mission would be explained in detail, questions answered, and everyone would go off knowing precisely what was expected of them and why. These men had no information, and the fact did not bother them at all.

American troops and transport were everywhere. On arriving at a road junction, vehicles of all kinds could be seen advancing north. Scout planes flew overhead and the sheer weight of men and machines was most comforting. That morning, I had pictured us as a spearhead advancing against determined opposition, but now I found myself part of a great tidal wave racing up the beach without a rock or breakwater in sight. In every town and village we were greeted by cheering crowds, lining both sides of the road shouting their acclamations. The expressions on their faces were wonderful to see. If we halted, even for a moment, they crowded about us, and hands would have to be shaken and faces kissed before we could pass on. It was an experience as incredible as it was enjoyable; only those who have known the like elsewhere can appreciate how we felt. This happy state of affairs continued until the early afternoon, when, after halting on the road for some minutes, as we had been doing from time to time all day, the order was given to take to the fields and spread out. While we were doing so, the shelling began. It was not so much the eventual explosions, as the dreadful whistle of the shells I found terrifying. Everyone lay down in their carriers while the drivers drove steadily on. Then the order was given to halt, and we leapt out of the truck and started digging fox-holes. A fox-hole was a shallow, narrow trench, just big enough for one man. I had a shovel, as did the others; but whereas they were soon lying sheltering from everything save a direct hit, I was still digging furiously at a miserable little hole, like a frustrated gold prospector. When they saw my plight my friends came to my rescue, and at a great risk to themselves – shells were now falling in salvos – dug my trench for me. I lay face downwards, my fingers in my ears, the ground quaking beneath me; but my fingers could not keep out the sound any more than my mind could ignore the thoughts passing through it. To die now seemed so unfair. After all, I had endured a little, escaped much, evaded capture for seven months, and now this! If I had still been with the Maquis a barrage would have been in the nature of things. I might have been just as frightened, but would have viewed dying differently; and the view one takes of dying is important: it affects the way one faces the prospect.

After about half an hour of preoccupation with my own thoughts and concern for my own safety, it dawned on me that my companions had just as much to endure as I had so, taking my courage in both hands, I peered bravely over the side of my fox-hole. The two good friends who had dug my trench were only a few yards away, and had extended their fox-holes to make a long single trench in which they could both lie end to end. I raised my head a little higher to see why they had done this, and saw they were playing dice.

My world back in perspective, the barrage lost some of its terrors.

The arrival of rocket-firing fighters put an end to the shelling and we continued our advance. As we were moving off, I overheard an American in another carrier say to his companion: 'That British lieutenant's a cool customer, he just lay down and had a nap.'

We continued advancing steadily till nightfall, then

halted in a wood. I tried to find out where we were and what was to happen next but no one knew anything.

'Just eat your supper, Lieutenant, and let the Army do the worrying,' said a friendly sergeant, and I could see how sensible an attitude this was for any infantryman to adopt. A barn served as a mess for all ranks, and those not on duty gathered there to eat their rations and have a smoke. I was continually being asked who I was by officers who came in, and got very tired of explaining.

No one was allowed to remove their helmets, so my painted gold bar always attracted their attention, and curiosity did the rest. Even these officers knew very little; they received orders and passed them on. Most of their orders came through on the radio; they could only acknowledge and obey – an infantryman is very much a pawn in the game of war. So indeed are all participants, but in the RAF, at any rate, we felt we were considered; an attempt was made to treat us as individual members of a team. The team was all-important, but the members mattered. In my experience, not many infantrymen felt the same applied to them.

Shelling began again, and everyone returned to their vehicles ready to move off if necessary. In fact, we did not move, but the occupants of my carrier, except the driver and myself, went out on patrol and did not return till morning. In a sense, they had a better night than we; for we lay under the truck enduring intermittent shelling, while they scouted round the countryside, without finding anything. I had offered to go with them, but was instructed to stay with the driver. Fortunately for me, the lieutenant in command of the patrol had interested himself in my problem, and the next morning took me to his colonel. The colonel was most understanding and arranged for me to go back to a supply depot which was being formed some miles behind our present position. He explained why the captain had been unable to send me back the previous morning. It appeared the troops in Septvaux had been the extreme edge of a fan-shaped movement which had spread out from the spearhead of the advance to help cover the flank of the main attack on Laon. Seeing his main force advancing so quickly and easily, and since the Germans were clearly only employing delaying tactics, the American commander had folded his fan and pushed it through the gap made by the point of his spearhead in order to exploit the situation to the full. Troops in reserve had, of course, been fanning out behind us, and had moved up in the night to broaden the front. As the colonel put it: 'The point of the dart of two days ago has become a flat sword.' The captain had not been able to send me back because there had been no position directly behind me. He would have had to send me to the centre of the advance before I could retreat. Since the line was advancing all the time this clearly was not practicable. As he had told me, if I had been a general he would have attempted to get me back, but as it was I was not important enough.

I said goodbye to my companions of the last twenty-four hours and left in a jeep for the depot. The roads were crowded with vehicles of all kinds, and the sheer weight of men and machines was, as it had been the day before, most impressive. On reaching the depot, which had not been there the previous day, it was amazing to see the degree of organization that had been established in a few hours. After a short wait, I saw the colonel, who was polite, but busy. He was, however, not only able to pass me on down the line, but actually had a truck going right through to Paris to pick up urgently required spares.

My driver was a man in the true tradition of truck-drivers. He was tall, thick-set and with enormous forearm muscles that would not have shamed Popeye. He had spent his adult life driving over the truck routes of the United States and was a most entertaining companion.

For some time we drove at a good speed, occasionally stopping at road junctions where American military police redirected us. We were heading for a depot where another driver was to take this truck on to Paris and my companion would 'rest up', as he put it. He had not been to bed for three days, he told me, and would be glad to get some sleep. He was speculating how far we were from the depot when, rounding a corner, we saw that a demonstration was going on in the village ahead. The driver slowed down, expecting the villagers to make way for us, but our truck was forced to stop by the milling crowd. We were puzzled as to what they were doing, but soon saw that their attention was focused on a young girl who sat on a stool crying, holding a baby on her knee. Behind her stood a tall fat man waving a large pair of scissors above his head, presumably indicating to the crowd what he was proposing to do. Suddenly with his left hand he pulled her long hair upwards with such force that she screamed in pain and rising to her feet let the baby roll off her knee on to the cobbled pavement, where the poor terrified child yelled pitifully. No one made any attempt to pick it up; the girl, not the baby, was the object of their attentions. A man grabbed the girl from behind and, against the upward pull the fat man still exerted on her hair, forced her down on to the stool again. As a result the fat man lost his hold and the girl was able to lean forward and try to pick up her baby, while blood ran from the torn roots in her head. But the man who had pulled her down prevented this by putting his arms round her and pulling her back. His hands were over her breasts, which he kneaded savagely.

'Thought you could escape, did you?' snarled the fat man, regaining his hold on her hair and pulling it back with such force that her tear-stained, anguished face was compelled to look upwards into his own. 'There is no escape. Thought you could love a German, did you?' He spat down on the upturned face, then thrust her from him and turned to the crowed. 'It is agreed, then, we shave her head?'

'No!' cried an angry voice. 'No! Have you all gone mad? Let this child go; it is for the authorities to decide whether she is a collaborator or not, not for you.' A thin and rather delicate-looking priest pushed his way through the crowd. He saw the baby lying on the ground and with a cry of dismay ran forward and picked it up. 'You have all gone mad,' he cried. 'You may be angry with the woman but not with the child.'

'It's a German's child,' said the fat man; 'it's not one of us.'

'We are all of one Father; don't let your reason leave you now that the day of liberation is here.'

'All this nonsense about one Father; what did He do for

us during the occupation? What did He do?' He gesticulated aggressively.

'I know it is a waste of time to argue with you. You Communists are all the same.' The priest handed the baby to a woman, then turned his attention to the man who held the girl on the stool. 'Let go of her. Look!' he cried to the crowd. 'See how he holds her! Is this not the man who has molested little children and once been driven from the village? Do you choose him and a Communist to lead you?'

The crowd was becoming openly divided. Many of them, particularly the women were clearly affected by what the priest was saying.

'That priest needs our help,' I said to the American.

He nodded, picked up his sten gun and we got down from the truck. As we moved through the crowd the fat man saw us and cried: 'Here are two Americans, they will see justice done.'

'Can we help you, Father?' I asked the priest, who had his back to me. He turned and a look of great relief came over his face.

'You speak French. This is marvellous; please explain to these people that they must not take the law into their own hands.'

'The Father is right,' I said. 'If she is to be punished, it will be after trial.'

'This is a French matter; it has nothing to do with Americans.'

It was clear the fat man was not going to give in easily. What was more, many people in the crowd still supported him. They were in a nasty mood, and I saw that short of opening fire there was no way we could prevent them torturing the girl.

'The Germans are up there,' shouted an angry man, pointing in the direction from which we had come. 'Why don't you go and fight them?'

The crowd audibly agreed with him and began forming up behind the big fat man and his mean-looking accomplice.

'Wait. In Heaven's name, wait.' The priest held his hands above his head. 'Listen to me.'

But they would not listen, and bore down on the

unfortunate girl, who fell to her knees in terror and flung her arms round the priest's legs. The pressure of the crowd was such that he would have overbalanced had I not supported him.

'Wait!' he kept shouting. 'Wait! Listen to reason.'

'We have listened long enough. This is not a Church affair. Now stand back or you will get hurt.' The big man held the back of his hand threateningly in front of the priest's face.

'I will not stand back; I know my duty.' The brave man stared his huge assailant straight in the eye.

Wham! The latter brought the back of his hand down with all his strength across the priest's face. I held him up as he recoiled from the savage blow. Before I could do anything, something flashed past my face, and there was a crack like the sound of a branch breaking in a high wind. There was a sudden silence, and the big Frenchman was lying on his back, his jaw askew, a bemused expression on his face. The American stood beside me, grimacing as he rubbed the knuckles of his right hand.

'Well, I guess that takes care of Fatso,' he drawled.

The sight of their leader prostrate on the ground with one of their liberators standing over him, their priest, blood running out of the side of his mouth and down his chin and tears in his eyes, the girl, her face deathly pale, the blood trickling down it from her head looking like red paint dripping on a white-washed wall, all this shocked them into silence; but not for long.

A general hubbub broke out.

'He should not have struck a priest.'

'This is no business of the Americans.'

'We can punish the girl if we wish.'

'That American must be strong.'

'Is Gaston dead?'

The efforts of Gaston's friends to rouse him were proving unsuccessful. The mean little pervert shouted: 'It will be a bad day for you, if he is dead.'

I did not attempt to answer, for just at that moment loud hooting announced the arrival of a jeep with three American Military police in it. Seeing me, and presuming I was an officer, the sergeant in charge jumped out and saluted.

This gesture had a profound effect on the crowd.

'He is an officer; now there will be trouble,' said one of the women who was attending to the priest.

I quickly explained the position to the sergeant. He looked across at the poor girl, a tragic sight as she sat alone weeping.

'We'll have to get her away from here. You say the kid is hers as well?'

'Yes, it is.'

'Primitive bastards!'

'We may have trouble moving her. The crowd's in a nasty mood.'

'What do you think we ought to do?'

'Let's ask the priest, he may have an idea.'

We walked over to the Father, who was sitting on the ground, attended by village women who were obviously upset.

'Are you all right, Father?' I asked.

'Yes,' he said with difficulty through his swollen lips.

'We want to move the girl. Do you think we'll have trouble?'

The women round him began to mutter angrily.

'Where will you take her?'

'I don't know, but somewhere safe.'

One of the women got up and ran over to the crowd round the still unconscious Gaston.

'They're going to take her away. She causes all this trouble and now they want to take her away.'

'Be ready to get the girl and baby into the truck,' I said to my companions. 'I'll try to pacify them.'

I walked over to the woman who was shouting. The priest, waving aside offers of assistance, got up and followed me.

'Please listen to me,' I said, ignoring the many interruptions. 'We'll take this girl with us and the charges against her will be investigated.'

'Investigated!' the woman laughed. 'What is there to investigate? She admits her child has a German father.'

'When your man struck Gaston it was because he had hit the Father. Gaston was wrong to do that. You can defend the Father but you cannot defend the girl.'

The crowd chorused their agreement with the old man who spoke.

I turned to the priest. 'Tell them, Father, there has been enough trouble already; we don't want any more.'

Speaking with difficulty the priest reiterated all I had said, but they took no notice and began shouting him down. I was now very concerned; it was quite impossible for us to leave the girl to the mercy of the mob, particularly after what had occurred. But what were we to do if they resisted? I owed my freedom to the French people; for seven months they had fed me, clothed me, sheltered me; how could I find myself in conflict with them? Yet I was in conflict, for no matter what she might have done, mob violence is no substitute for fair trial.

'We are taking her with us,' I said arbitrarily, 'and I advise you not to hinder us.'

If the fat Gaston had been conscious, my bluff would never have worked; as it was, however, they had no leader. Gaston's principal accomplice was too cowardly to do more than shout from the midst of the crowd, and there were no young men present. Indeed, with the exception of the two principals, the crowd was composed of women and elderly men. In retrospect it is not difficult to see why Gaston had such influence over them.

I beckoned to the sergeant to move the girl and her baby to the truck. He passed on the order, then walked over and stood beside me facing the crowd. He was immaculately turned out, and his fine build and bearing lent authority to my remarks. They watched in sullen silence while one American helped the stumbling girl and another carried her baby. We heard the truck start up, then the jeep. The jeep drove up beside us. Without turning round the sergeant spoke to the driver: 'Signal them to move on; it'll be easier for us to leave when she has gone.'

The truck revved up and drove past us and away down the road.

The crowd muttered bitterly but there was no demonstration. I turned to the priest. 'You had better come with us, Father; it may not be safe for you to stay here.'

'Safe for me to stay here! This is my parish.'

'I know, but after what has happened today ...'

'After what has happened today, it is vital that I stay. There is work for me to do.'

I was going to argue further but he took my hand and shook it. 'You'd better leave now; you are not popular.'

'But someone must look after you, Father!'

'Someone does,' he said, and then hurried over to the now conscious Gaston to see if there was anything he could do to help.

At the next depot, the problem of what to do with the girl was solved by the girl herself. She told me she had relations in Eastern France if she could only get there. Money was found, arrangements made, and so far as I know this was the end of an unhappy story.

I am not approving this girl's conduct. The French people, in their own minds, were still at war with Germany, and looked on anyone who collaborated with their oppressors as a traitor. Nevertheless, even allowing for the fact that the girl had been a German soldier's mistress and had borne his child, she was no more than twenty years old, and the French, of all people, should know that the heart recognizes no barriers – that is, if history is to be believed. The village priest, who, presumably, knew all the circumstances of the case, and certainly could not have condoned her conduct, thought his parishioners wrong to torture her, and had therefore intervened.

This question of collaboration was often misrepresented. If a man was in a responsible position and in constant contact with the German and Vichy authorities it was extremely difficult for him to participate in Resistance affairs. That many men so placed did, in fact, participate is all to their credit; that many did not, does not mean that they were necessarily collaborators. The man of little importance had a far better chance of avoiding detection. Then there were those who were 'on the run', men who had forged papers, or no papers; it was both necessary and easy for them to be active in some Maquis group. The men who chose to disappear in order to avoid being sent to Germany as conscripted workers, or who had fallen foul of the authorities and been compelled to take to the woods, were really outlaws. That they served the Allied cause splendidly is readily acknowledged, but the life they led did fit into the consequences of their chosen existence. The man who could not disappear without abandoning his family, and who knew that if he carried on with his job he could assure them a reasonable standard of living, should not be condemned for remaining neutral. If he co-operated actively with the enemy, it was a different story, but many did not; they were only too ready to help their compatriots, but either through lack of opportunity or perhaps courage were never able to reveal their patriotism. In saying this, I am not detracting from the praise due to the wonderfully brave men of the Maquis. All that I am saying is that it is wrong to condemn, out of hand, a man who may not have made a tangible contribution to his nobler brothers' efforts.

All men are not equal either in terms of courage or motive, and this applied both inside and outside the Resistance movement. For a short while one had only to point a finger and shout 'Collaborator!' and the crowd were ready to stone the accused. They would have been often better employed examining the credentials of his accuser.

Thirteen

Soon after leaving the village we changed drivers. The new driver was not a talkative man, and for most of the journey we travelled in silence. His reticence was welcome to me, and, while he chain-smoked, I sat contentedly by his side enjoying the drive, the scenery and a feeling of well-being. We passed through Laon, Soissons, Villers-Cotterets and then, instead of following the Nanteuil-Dammartin route and entering Paris from the north, were directed by Military police through the forest of Domaniale and on to Meaux, where we stopped and refuelled. There was plenty of evidence of recent fighting in the towns we passed through: abandoned tanks, field guns, troop carriers and so on. Children still stood by the edge of the road cheering and waving to every vehicle; but the adult population was back at work and hardly spared the passing troops a glance. Yet only a few days previously they had received them in a near-delirium of excitement. Life has to return to normal, of course, but I was glad to have experienced the drive of the previous day through newly liberated territory.

While the truck was being refuelled, I spoke to an old man who was sitting on a seat sunning himself. To my surprise he asked me if I were British. On learning that I was, he told me he had worked in London for seven years before the first world war. 'I knew that accent was not American,' he said.

I would have liked to talk to him longer, but we had to be on our way.

An hour later we entered Paris.

We drove into an enormous depot. I sought out the commanding officer and told him I wished to make contact with the British authorities. This officer was not helpful or even pleasant, but did tell me where British Military police could be found. He did not offer me transport and in view of his attitude I did not ask for it, but walked a couple of miles in the fading light to the Army police post. Despite the instructions the American had given me I would not have found it but for the help of a friendly young Frenchman. By now I was very tired and longed for a bath and a good night's rest, but on seeing the sergeant in charge of the post something warned me that here was another obstacle on the path to freedom.

He was a big man with large thick hands, a bullet-shaped, closely-cropped head, and an extra-ordinarily unintelligent face. Two pink eyes peered out over a broken nose, and his thick ears suggested that his punch-drunk expression might be founded on fact.

'Sir,' he said, getting up with the air of a man who was not over-impressed by American officers.

'Good evening, Sergeant,' I said pleasantly. 'Despite this uniform, I am actually an RAF pilot officer and I would like to see the Provost Marshal.'

'Eh!' was his comment.

I repeated my request.

He looked at the two corporals who were in the room with him and were now taking an interest, and then back at me.

To be confronted by three such vacant expressions was almost overpowering, but I tried again.

'You see, I was shot down seven months ago and have been in hiding ever since. The Americans liberated me the day before yesterday and I have just arrived in Paris. I want to get back to England and am sure your Provost Marshal could help me.'

' 'E's not 'ere.'

'Oh, where is he?'

'Don't know!'

'What do you mean, you don't know? Come on, Sergeant!'

I was getting angry and impatient.

'Afore we go on much further I'd better see yer identity card,' he said dryly.

'I haven't got an identity card. You must know aircrew don't carry them in action. I have no means of identification; you'll just have to take my word.'

' 'Ow do I know yer not 'aving me on?'

'Because, my dear man, I am asking to see your superior officer. I'm not trying to escape. I'm in effect giving myself up.'

'He's got a point there,' said one of the corporals wisely, and the sergeant nodded his concurrence.

'Well, sir, even allowing for all that, there's not much we can do. Our officer's away since yesterday mornin' and I dunno when 'e'll be back. There are no British troops proper like in Paris. I dunno where to send you.'

This was really too much, and for a moment I was at a loss for words. Then I saw a telephone on the sergeant's desk and had an idea.

'Sergeant, let me see your telephone directory.'

'Why, sir?'

'So that I can see if there's anyone we might ring up who could help me.'

'I'm sorry, sir. It's confidential information.'

I was so sure now that my problem could be solved that I was not annoyed.

'Well, Sergeant, would you look down the list and tell me if there is anyone there who might help a British airman?'

He nodded, and taking a piece of cardboard on to which a sheet of paper had been pasted scanned it carefully. He looked up. 'The British Embassy?' he said hopefully.

'Just the thing. Will you get them?'

The call had apparently to pass through an American switchboard and it was some minutes before we got through.

'It's ringing now,' he beamed.

'Good, would you like me to speak to them?'

'No, I'll speak.' His tone was rather hurt. We waited for fully five minutes but no one answered. He put the phone down despondently. 'There's no'un there; must 'ave gone 'ome.'

'Where's home?'

'Arrr! If we knew that we'd know where to send you. As it is, Paris is a big place.'

An awkward silence followed, during which no one could think of anything to say. Quite obviously my arrival had disturbed the equanimity of their existence and without their officer they did not know what to do.

'Well, I'd better go and find somewhere to sleep!' My remark begged an answer but none was forthcoming.

'I'll call on the Embassy tomorrow; there'll probably be someone there if I don't go too early. Good night, Sergeant, thank you for your help.'

'It was nothing, sir. Any time.'

He beamed reassuringly and followed me to the door.

'My hofficer will be sorry 'e's missed you, sir. Very strange his being away like this. Can't understand it.'

'He's found a bit of stuff somewhere. I hope she's worth it. Tell him from me ...' I stopped. After all, there was no way of knowing what the man was doing; it might be important. Who could blame him for not telling his NCOs everything. But the sergeant was nodding wisely. 'Wimmin can take up a lot of time, and cost a lot of money. Good night, sir.' And with that he more or less closed the door in my face.

My problem as to what to do next was solved by the young Frenchman who had helped me find the MP post.

'Can I be of further assistance?'

His tone was so pleasant, his demeanour so helpful, that I was uncharitable enough to think he must have some ulterior motive.

'Could you direct me to an hotel?'

'An hotel?' he asked incredulously. 'But why?'

'Because, my friend, I must have somewhere to sleep.'

'Do you mean to tell me your soldiers have no accommodation for you?'

'None.'

'But this is ridiculous; you must come home with me.'

I put up a token resistance, but was too tired to argue with so persistent and charitable a young man.

His father owned a barber's shop, and not only did he give me food and shelter but a shave and haircut as well. These good people did everything they could to make me comfortable, and it was odd to reflect that even now I had made contact with my own nationals I was still dependent on French charity. My attempts to pay the barber for his kindness were firmly refused. He even offered me accommodation for as long as I might remain in Paris.

After a good supper, I slept soundly until late the next morning. Breakfast, a shave, a haircut and an early lunch followed in that order. Then I bade my friends goodbye and headed for the British Embassy in the Rue St Honoré. I stopped an American jeep and got a lift as far as the Champs Élysées where a BBC correspondent's truck was parked. A man I believe to have been Richard Dimbleby was standing in it wearing a war correspondent's armband. Feeling here was someone who might, at any rate, give me information, I approached him, but the truck drove off, and though I ran after it and shouted, Dimbleby only waved a friendly acknowledgement. With the aid of a gendarme I found the Embassy and was going in when an American corporal came up to me.

'Say, bud, can you tell me where to find these French prostitutes?'

'Not in here, Corporal, this is the British Embassy.'

'Say! You mean this is off limits to Americans? How come the limeys get all the fun?'

'No. No. Corporal, this is an Embassy.'

'Hell! What's in a name! Once you've paid over your dough it's the same in any language.'

He then caught sight of the gold bar on my helmet for the first time.

'Sorry, sir, didn't see your rank, sir, but with respect, sir, is there an American Embassy?'

'Yes, of course.'

He brightened. 'Say, sir, can you direct me?'

As it happened I could, having passed it earlier. I have sometimes wondered what happened when he got there.

In the Embassy I found three paratrooper NCOs drinking tea. I told them who I was and immediately received a cup myself and the reassuring information that there would be accommodation for me in the Hotel Westminster. There were, it was good to hear, other airmen in the same position as myself, and it was likely we would be leaving in the morning for Bayeux on our way home.

Two Army officers came in while we were talking. They took me into their office and not only confirmed all the sergeant had said, but authorized the necessary procedure. Whether they had lunched particularly well or were simply overcome with joy at finding themselves in Paris, I don't know, but they were two of the jolliest people imaginable.

After a wash and a brush-up at the hotel, the paratroopers and I went out on the town. I had plenty of money, having received a share of the money dropped, from time to time, to the Maquis from British planes. At the time I had not thought much about it, having nothing to spend money on – but now! …

Sitting in a café on the Champs Élysées, looking up towards the unlit Arc de Triomphe, my thoughts went to my companions of a few hours ago. Where were they now? Were they lying in fox-holes enduring another bombardment? Or perhaps out on patrol losing another night's sleep? Wherever they were, or whatever they were doing, I raised my glass to them. And my good friends of the Maquis, were they all liberated yet? Had Bob and the others found any Germans to fight? If so, let God be with them. Dr and Madame Boury and Jacqueline, had they now the freedom they so richly deserved? Then all the others, back to Madame Leroux and the brave farmer of Lor! I raised my glass again. Could it be, perhaps, that, inspired by their example, I might myself so serve my fellow men and women one day that someone, somewhere, would raise a metaphorical glass to me or my memory, and feel towards me the same warmth and gratitude I had now for these others?

We moved from café to café. We watched a cabaret. We sang. We danced. And, by two o'clock in the morning, my guests (it was my party), had found other friends and I was alone looking for the Hotel Westminster.

Fourteen

'Have you a light?' asked the girl on the corner.

I fumbled in my pockets, found a match and lit her cigarette. By its flickering flame she appeared to be pretty. What she was and what she sought was obvious; for I had already lost my three friends to her kind; but she spoke pleasantly and made no attempt to thrust herself on me. Not that I had any intention of allowing her to; if I had wanted that sort of thing there had been plenty of occasions already during the evening. My three friends had succumbed to the charms of other ladies, but I was not going to. Within a few hours I hoped to be in London, and had no wish to take *un souvenir d'amour* with me. To my question as to the whereabouts of the Hotel Westminster she was vague. She fancied she had heard the name but did not know the locality. This was obviously not true; it was simply that she wanted me to accompany her to her room.

'Mademoiselle, you must know its whereabouts. It is a well-known hotel.'

'No, I don't know, but why don't you come to the hotel where I am staying?'

'Hotel?'

'Yes, it is an hotel; if you want a room to yourself it can be arranged.'

'Let's not play about, mademoiselle; girls do not stand in the street at this time of the night for no reason.'

'That's true,' she said mournfully. 'I must find a man before I can go home, and I'm tired.'

'Then why not go home?'

'I dare not; the woman who employs me would be angry.'

'You work for a brothel?'

'Yes.'

'Why?'

'A girl must eat. My parents are dead.'

I did not believe a word of this and told her so.

'Believe what you will, but I don't know where the Hotel Westminster is, and I can't go home.'

There was a ring of truth in her voice and I softened a little. 'I will pay you to take me to the Hotel Westminster, then you can go back to Madame with the money and tell her that you found an American who didn't want to stay the night.'

She laughed. 'Honestly, I do not know the Hotel Westminster.'

'Then it looks as if we must both spend the night here.'

'If we are to spend it together why not in my room?'

'Because I do not want to go to bed with you.'

'Is it because you love your wife?'

'Yes,' I said, feeling that if that was a reason she could understand it would do as well as any other.

She sighed. 'It must be nice to have a man who feels that way about you.'

We stood in silence for a moment while a distant clock chimed twice.

'It's two o'clock. Why not just come home with me. So long as you pay me, I'll be happy. You'll have a bed for the night, and I'll have the money.'

What she said was true, so feeling it was that or nothing I reluctantly agreed.

She took me to what appeared to be a small hotel. Despite the lateness of the hour the lounge was fairly well filled with Americans and girls sitting round little coffee tables.

'Let's have a drink.' She indicated a vacant table.

We sat down and were served by a portly old man who grinned slyly as he set a bottle and two glasses before us.

'It is good for love,' he said in English and was about to add something, no doubt in French, when she interrupted him: 'Monsieur speaks French.'

He forced a smile. 'How unusual; Monsieur is the first American to come here who does.'

He waited until I had paid for the bottle and tipped him and then shuffled off.

'He's an old crook; he would have charged you a stupid price for the bottle had I not spoken.'

I could not help laughing. 'Like I'm paying for the bed!'

She smiled, and for the first time I appreciated how very pretty she was, as indeed were many of the girls in the room.

'Why do you do this. It is all so very unnecessary.'

'We do it because the money is good and easy and you cannot say it is unnecessary. Look at your comrades!'

I looked and saw what she meant. We went up to a small bedroom most of which was taken up by a iron-posted double bed.

'Do you have to sleep here?' I inquired.

'Of course, it is my room, but you can have the bed; I'll sleep on the floor, unless,' she added slyly, 'you've changed your mind.'

'I've not changed my mind, but I'll sleep on the floor; you can have the bed.'

'For five hundred francs you are entitled to the bed.'

'And other things. But if I give up one I can give up the other.'

I pulled the eiderdown off the bed, took a pillow and a blanket and made myself comfortable on the floor.

'But this is ridiculous, there is plenty of room in the bed. Let us be sensible!'

'Mademoiselle, I'm the most sensible man you've met for a long time – good night.' I turned my back on her and went to sleep, ignoring remarks about how soft the mattress was and how stupid chaste Americans were who slept on the floor. She felt my behaviour was an insult to her profession.

I had arranged for the old man to call me at eight o'clock, for the coach was due at the Hotel Westminster at ten. Two hours would be sufficient to enable me to find the hotel in daylight, I felt sure. I did not sleep well; the floor, with only an eiderdown between me and it, was very hard, added to which the girl snored dreadfully. When the old man's knocking wakened me, it put an end to a most uncomfortable night. His vast experience in these matters had taught him that a bowl of strong black coffee was so welcome to most of his clients in the morning that they tipped generously. He thrust one through the door to me and was suitably rewarded. It was nectar.

The girl appeared to be still asleep but, when I put the bowl down and made to leave, she opened her eyes and sat up 'Thank you for being so kind,' she said.

I closed the door quietly behind me, and was about to walk along the landing to the staircase, when the door of the room opposite opened, and a tall, thin American backed out waving a hand to the someone he was leaving. He stopped when half out of the room and leant on the door.

' 'Bye, honey,' he said, and blew a kiss in the direction of the bed, the foot of which I could just see.

' 'Bye, sweetheart. Some other time, huh?'

There was no answer, but there was evidently some sort of response, for he giggled stupidly.

'Just do that one more time, baby, and I'll come back and do something about it.'

I coughed politely.

He spun round.

'What the hell?' he exclaimed.

'Good morning,' I said.

'What are you snooping about for?' He looked ready for a fight.

'Snooping about? I'm just leaving my room.'

'You been sleeping in there?'

'Yes.'

'Sorry, bud; thought you was snooping on me. We had quite a party last night. Don't feel too good right now. Guess another cup of coffee would help. Let's go find some.'

We started to walk to the staircase. A cistern flushed, a door opened, and a girl in a dressing-gown came out and walked downstairs.

'That's a good idea,' said the American and went into the bathroom.

I waited for him at the top of the stairs. The girl who had just gone down came up again with a middle-aged Frenchman. They passed me without speaking, a most unusual occurrence in France, and went into a bedroom. The day shift had taken over. The American came out and we went downstairs, passing another couple on the way.

'Say!' he said. 'Civilians come here!'

'Of course they do. Another couple came up while I was waiting for you.'

'That's funny! Didn't see any last night.'

'These will be regulars. The fellows you saw last night had all been picked up.'

'Like you and me.' He nudged me in the ribs.

I suddenly felt very prudish and resented his inference; however, before I could say anything a plaintive voice cried out from behind one of the doors: 'Oh, come on honey.'

The American nudged me again.

'Some guys ain't never had enough.'

'Let's get out of here,' I said. 'I've had enough.'

'What's wrong with this place? It's OK.'

'For you, perhaps.'

'Wait a minute. What gives with you, bud? You didn't have to spend the night here. You came like I did, 'cause you wanted a dame.'

'I didn't, as it happens.'

'What you come for, then?'

'It's a long story.'

'I've plenty of time.'

'Look, I've got to find the Westminster Hotel.'

'Why?'

'Because that's where I'm billeted.'

I walked ahead of him and out into the street, hoping he would leave me and go and look for the coffee he said he needed. But after hesitating for a moment he ran after me and put a restraining hand on my shoulder.

'Just a minute. What gives with you?'

'Nothing. I want to find my hotel.'

'That's a funny accent you got. Are you an American?'

'No, I'm not.'

'Then what are you?'

I explained. He looked at me incredulously.

'Then your spending the night here was accidental?'

'Yes, quite accidental.'

'Accidents like that never happen to me; if I was lost no dame would come along and take me home to bed.'

Again a feeling of resentment came over me. Not that I was in any way puritanical, but the atmosphere of love for sale that pervaded the brothel was not something I could enjoy.

'I didn't sleep with the girl; I merely shared her room.'

He grinned nastily. 'Who are you kidding?'

'I'm not kidding anyone.'

I now regretted my outburst. It would have been far better to have let him think what he wanted to think and not to start a stupid argument.

'You're a ...' He stopped and stared past me. 'Hell, here's trouble!'

Three jeeps stopped in line alongside us. A captain was sitting in the first one.

'What do you men think you're doing?' he shouted.

'Doing, sir?' said my companion in a puzzled tone.

'Yes – doing. Your heads are uncovered and your dress is a disgrace.'

The American put on his helmet and began zipping up his jacket. I walked forward to the captain.

'I think I'd better explain ...'

'Put on your helmet,' he said.

I put on my helmet and he saw my gold bar. For a moment he was embarrassed and hesitant. Taking advantage of his confusion I went on: 'I'm a British officer. I've been in this country for several months and this uniform was given to me by men of the Third Armoured Division of your Ninth Army who liberated me. I'm looking for the Westminster Hotel, and would be grateful if you could tell me where it is.'

He remained silent for a moment, eyeing me up and down, then said: 'Have you any means of identification?'

'None, but you can check my story with the British Embassy. The IC troops there billeted me at the Westminster. I'm hoping to fly home today.'

He was thoughtful for a minute: 'Supposing your story is true, and I'm not saying it isn't, what are you doing here?'

'I slept in there last night.'

'In there?' He pointed to the brothel.

'Yes. I couldn't find my hotel.'

'How did you find this one?'

'Well, it's rather a long story.'

'I'll bet it is. Tell me about it.'

'Now, look, Captain, I've told you who I am, you can easily check my story; what's it to you where I slept last night?'

He grinned, much amused at my embarrassment.

'Look, son, what you say may be true, but so far as I'm concerned you're wearing a uniform you admit you're not entitled to wear and that warrants an investigation. I can do one of two things. I can take you back to the post and have your story checked; or, if you story is feasible, I can run you to the Westminster Hotel.'

'You know it?'

'Oh, sure.'

'Excuse me, sir,' said a sergeant. 'This soldier,' he indicated my companion, 'shall we hold him?'

The captain thought for a moment. 'Do you know him?' he asked me.

'No, we just met. I was asking him if he knew where the Westminster was.'

He nodded. 'Find out what you can, Sergeant. If he's OK let him go.'

The captain did not look like a man who would be lenient; but at the moment I was much more interesting than a soldier with his jacket unzipped.

'Now, let's see,' he said. 'You couldn't find your hotel. What did you do, then?'

'Well, while I was looking a girl asked me if I had a match.'

'She what?'

'She asked me if I had a match.'

He leaned back in his seat and pushed his helmet up a fraction; his driver turned his face away from me.

'Please go on.'

'As it happened, I had a match so lit her cigarette.'

'Nice of you. And then?'

'I asked her if she knew where the Westminster Hotel was.'

'Don't go on,' he said, holding up his hand. 'She didn't know.'

'She said she didn't.'

'Holy cow! And you believed her?'

'No, not really.'

Before I could go on he held up his hand again. 'Now tell me if this is right. She suggested you went home with her?'

'What is the use of my going on – you won't believe me.'

'Try me,' he said, grinning good-humouredly. His driver blew his nose furiously and the sergeant, having got rid of the American, now joined the audience.

'So I spent the night in there.' I pointed at the brothel.

'With her?'

'Not with her.'

'How come?'

'Look, I'm hoping to go home today. I don't want to spend my leave in hospital.'

'O.K. But how did you get rid of her?'

'I wouldn't have anything to do with her.'

'So she went away after giving you the key to her room?'

'Oh, where's all this getting you? You know I'm British.'

'Tell me, did you pay her anything?'

'For the room, yes.'

'Ah! But not for anything else?'

'Nothing else.'

'Just one more thing. Don't tell me you slept on the floor, and she in the bed?'

I was silent for a minute, then laughed: 'Come on, take me to the Westminster.'

'Oh, brother!' he said. 'That's the least I can do.'

I handed my key in at the Westminster Hotel and joined the party waiting for the coach. They were a mixed bag; some Air Force, some Army. None of them had been in France more than a few weeks, some only a few days. The Army representatives were paratroopers and infantrymen, most of whom had been taken prisoner but liberated by the advancing Americans before they could be moved to Germany. One Army officer had been hidden by a French family for some weeks, and was very proud of a diary he had kept recording all that had happened during that time. He was very hurt when I told him it was a damnable thing to do. The thought of what would have happened to his helpers if that diary had fallen into the wrong hands made me livid.

We flew from Le Bourget to Bayeux in a Dakota. Remembering my last mission, it was no fun flying without a parachute. We all expected to go on to England after lunch, but although we actually got into an aircraft it never took off. No satisfactory reason was given. I suppose the Dakota was wanted for some other duty. When I expressed my views about the delay a little too forcefully, the dispatching officer solemnly told me that since I had had no aircrew medical for six months I was really ineligible to fly anyway. My answer to this made him very cross. We were moved to a house in Bayeux, and went under canvas in the garden.

An Intelligence officer interviewed us. The fact that I

had come from so far north meant he had to find out whether St Gobain had been liberated yet before he could tell me that any information I might have was now useless. The extra work displeased him. Everyone was fed up at having to spend another night in France. And when, a rather aggrieved company, we went out that evening, we quarrelled with a bumptious Guard's officer who told one of the other ranks in the party that he was improperly dressed. A short altercation followed during which this gentleman lost his temper and his trousers; when our Army companions left him, he was in no position to press his charge further. I was not directly involved in this fracas, but later on was more or less arrested myself while watching an ENSA concert party. It was again a Guard's officer who thought I looked suspicious in my rather worse for wear American battledress. I explained and, when a telephone call had confirmed my story, the officer apologized. Nevertheless, it was infuriating to be hauled out of the stalls like a wanted criminal.

The next day, we crossed the Channel in a corvette instead of flying home. Although we embarked in the afternoon, we did not put to sea till after dark. Partly to pass the time, I ate an enormous meal and have never regretted anything so much. The Channel was rough, the journey to Newhaven took some hours, and the corvette pitched and tossed all over the place. I was so ill that, if we had been torpedoed, there was little I could have done to save myself. When we arrived, I had to be helped ashore. After changing our French money into English, which caused some fuss because I had more than I was supposed to have, we boarded a train for London. It was not a special train and the travelling public took a great interest in us and our curious mixture of uniforms. The story got round that we were repatriated prisoners of war and people crowded the corridors to peer at us. I was still feeling very ill and, lying back in my seat with my eyes closed, was more or less oblivious to the world. Suddenly a woman cried out: 'Oh, that poor young American, he looks like death!' And people pressed forward to see. I raised my head and offered a sickly grin, hoping thereby to dispel their fears. All my gesture did was to evoke a murmur of sympathy. 'Isn't he brave?' someone said. My companions enjoyed my discomfiture as much as these well-meaning people enjoyed seeing what was to them a 'bit of the real thing' – someone straight from a concentration camp. The story that we were repatriated prisoners was echoed down the platform at Waterloo, and a generous young man thrust several pound notes on to one of our party asking him to buy us all drinks.

On arriving at the Air Ministry (the Army men had gone to the War Office), we were told to write a report covering the period we had been missing and this I did on a single sheet of foolscap.

'Is this all?' asked the WAAF officer.

'Isn't it enough?'

'Well, you've been missing seven months!'

'What else do you want to know. I've mentioned where I was, what I did, and the names of the people who helped me. There isn't much else I can say.'

She smiled sympathetically. 'Let me put it this way: whether you receive some recognition or not may depend on this report.'

'You mean what I may have done is not so important as what I say I've done.'

'Of course not; every statement will be checked. It's just that you might elaborate a little.'

'In effect, shoot a line!'

She laughed. 'Have it your own way; it's your report.'

I felt uncomfortable. She was obviously trying to help me. Yet surely all Intelligence wanted were the bare facts without elaboration. I said as much and she agreed, but went on: 'You give no details of the various occasions you operated this radio you refer to. There must be a lot you could say about that alone!'

'I could, but I want to go home tonight. It may sound silly, but that means more to me at the moment than anything else.'

'I understand,' she said; 'it's only that I've had some experience of these things and feel you might add to what you've said with advantage.'

I suppose I could have done, but with advantage to whom? To Intelligence? No! They had the facts. If they wanted more information, it was easy enough for them to ask for it. To myself? Perhaps! But that depends on how highly one values recognition. At that particular moment, my mind was set on getting home that evening, and nothing else mattered very much. That is not to say I was contemptuous of recognition. If some had come my way, it would have been nice to know that my little contribution had been acknowledged, but whether it was or not was for others to decide. They had the facts – which could be checked – and if facts are to be checked no preliminary embellishment should be necessary.

A medical examination followed and I was given an extra three weeks' leave on medical grounds. There was nothing seriously wrong with me but my weight was under ten stone, and a kindly MO thought additional rest and double rations would do no harm. This, added to the three weeks' leave everyone was granted, offered the prospect of a good long holiday. We did not complete all the formalities that day and were told to return on the morrow, but those of us who lived in the Home Counties were allowed to go home for the night, and thankfully I went.

No service transport was available for those of us who were going home, so I left the Air Ministry building in Kingsway, walked round Aldwych, across the Strand and over Waterloo Bridge to the station. By the time I arrived there I was feeling very self-conscious; my scruffy appearance was attracting attention. As soon as I entered the station two large American MPs stopped me.

'Where's your hat, soldier?' one of them demanded.

For a moment I hesitated. Did I really have to start explaining who and what I was all over again. My hesitation was fatal. Satisfied that I was a deserter, a drunk, or both, they frog-marched me at high speed to their police post. It was a humiliating experience, for the station was crowded, and an arrested man is always an object of interest. The bored-looking people who had sat on the long seats with which the platforms abounded had the best view, for we marched down the corridor made by their benches: a convenient route for the police – a gauntlet for me.

'We've got him,' said one of my escorts to the staff sergeant who stood behind the counter. 'Caught him as he came into the station.'

'That's not him,' said the sergeant.

'It's not?'

'No, look again.' He passed over a photograph. My

escorts – they were both corporals – looked at it carefully.

'He's right,' said one of them. 'That's not him.'

They all looked at me.

'Well, you don't owe him an apology, anyway,' said the sergeant. 'Come on, soldier, let's see your papers.' He held out his hand.

'Before we go any further I want to see the officer in charge of this post. A case of mistaken identity is one thing, but not giving a man time to establish his identity is another. Before I could tell these men who I was they forced me to march here, humiliating me in front of all those people outside. I am a British officer given this uniform by men of the Third Division of your Ninth Army who liberated me in occupied France. Here are my papers.' I banged a pass – that I had been given before leaving the Air Ministry – on the counter. He looked at it, then at the two corporals.

'You arrested the officer here without asking to see his papers first?'

'Well, we thought …'

'You what!' He looked at them both despairingly.

'We thought …'

'You thought, did you. You, you …' Lost for words, he stood gesticulating helplessly, then he turned to me. 'What can I say, sir? These men …' He looked so miserable I intervened. After all, this was a happy day for me. Now that I had established my identity there was really no need to go any further. At first, I had been angry at my public humiliation; but now, suddenly, I felt sorry for the two men who had, after all, been doing only what they thought was their duty.

'Let's forget it, Sergeant. I lost my temper for a moment then. But … well, let's forget it.'

'You don't want to see our PM.'

'No. I don't want to see him.'

We all shook hands.

'How about a drink?' I said.

'I can't leave the post, sir, but I reckon these two can. They owe you a drink.' The two corporals took off their armbands. We left the post and walked to the buffet, walked down the same corridor of long seats, past the same staring, now mystified, faces and into the buffet. On the last seat sat a middle-aged Cockney, the first world war ribbons on his waistcoat peeping round his unbuttoned coat.

'Gawd strewth!' he said. 'What an army.'

Our drink was enlivened by the barmaid, who gave us a dramatic and highly improbable account of a flying bomb incident of the previous evening. When she had finished I mentioned the fact that I had never seen one. 'Never seen one!' She stopped in the middle of drawing a pint and stared at me incredulously.

'No, I've never seen one.'

She shrugged her shoulders: 'Well, it's what I've always thought. This is a civilians' war. You blokes in uniform don't do nuffink.'

We left the buffet. I said goodbye to the Americans; bought my ticket and headed for home, feeling an empty compartment would be an advantage if I were to get there without further incident.

The train from Waterloo to Richmond seemed to take an interminable time, but when at last it arrived I did not catch a bus to the bottom of Richmond Hill as I could have done, but walked slowly through the town. There was evidence of bomb damage, but otherwise the main street was much the same as it had been seven months before. A small queue stood outside the Odeon and as I passed a soldier laughed to his girlfriend: 'Don't you know there's a war on?'

I crossed the road, walked down on to Richmond Bridge and looked up and then down the river. The evening was fine and warm, the towpaths crowded. How nice the girls looked in their summer dresses! A police launch passed underneath, a tug hooted, and the ducks near the bank bobbed up and down in the swell like coloured corks. It was good to be home.

I left the bridge and walked slowly up Richmond Hill. Near the top, I turned into the forecourt of the block of flats where my parents lived. Just as I was about to go in someone called my name. I looked up and saw a friend of my mother's. 'Oh, Lionel,' she said, 'you're back! Your mother *will* be pleased.'

Postscript

After my leave was over I was posted to Nutts Corner in Northern Ireland for a conversion course onto York transport planes. One day my Commanding Officer sent for me and told me to report to a Colonel Aymour at Room 055, the War Office in Whitehall. He said there was to be no mention to anyone of the reason for my visit when I returned.

Greatly intrigued, I duly reported to the Colonel. After asking me some questions he brought up the question of Soisson, in a rather offhand way: 'Give me your version of what happened,' he said.

I told my story at some length. When I had finished he made no comment but went on to question me on other matters relating to my stay in France.

There were questions about the Bourys and, in particular, Bob. He took some notes and then, preserving the formality between a senior and a junior officer, told me I could return to my squadron.

Before leaving I asked, 'Could you tell me, Sir, how agents in France could have had access to my personal file unless our Intelligence Service was involved?'

He hesitated, then spoke tersely, 'You were told to report here to answer questions not to ask them.'

Military discipline ensured that that was the end of our conversation. But I wonder still, why he could not give me an answer, unless it was that no military service can ever admit that any of its men are expendable.